GRAHAM CRIST + JOHN DOYLE

SUPER TIGHT

MODELS FOR LIVING AND MAKING CULTURE IN DENSE URBAN ENVIRONMENTS

Edited By TOM MURATORE

ACTAR, Barcelona
RMIT School of Architecture & Urban Design

Contents

Ủ TÍU
HAY
Ổ ĐỀ
UẾ CHAY
CHO VAY
0902.352.131
CHO VAY
TRẢ GÓP
0902.352.131
CHO VAY
TRẢ GÓP
0902.352.131

TY TNHH THƯƠNG MẠI - DỊCH VỤ - XÂY DỰNG
CÁC LOẠI KÍNH NHÔM CAO CẤP
ĐỨC THU
PHỤ K
Chuyên cun
- Bản lề sà
- Trụ cầu th
- Decal, gi
Địa chỉ: 52
Đt: 0938 42
59-F1 643.72
59-U2 105.09

The *super tight* refers to the small, intense, robust and hyper-condensed city spaces that emerge as a by-product of extreme urban density. *Tightness* is a consequence of density, but is not density itself, as commonly understood. It is a series of social, economic and cultural practices that have developed in cities as a response to rapid growth and urban consolidation.

At another scale, *tightness* can be measured and quantified in the architectural models that act as urban infill and the backdrop for these practices to continue. The Super Tight project investigates the cultures that have emerged in dense cities, particularly in Asia over the past thirty years, and the role that designers play in the material and social behaviours of *tightness*. To be *tight* is to be small and constrained, but also to be in sync with existing conditions, to be open to the economy and the social intimacy of being close. Through qualitative observations, this project argues for the benefits of urban closeness and very high density. It aims to unpack and convey both the delight and difficulty that emerges through this close occupation in large cities.

There is a relationship between our physical footprint and the consumption of ecological resources. However inexact that correlation, a *tighter* city consumes less. There is also a loose relationship between a city's density and its built volume; the densest cities are usually not the tallest. The rapidly growing large cities of Asia are critical for understanding our future footprint. If only by the weight of population, and scale of transformation, they provide the key insights into current ways of being densely urbanised. The by-product of an unprecedented metropolitan expansion and unprecedented shifts in patterns of consumption will be new urban models and new architectures; new models for living and making culture laid over old patterns. Transformations in the technologies of transport, production or communications as well as the pressures of economics and ecologies may radically *tighten* cities. The evidence of the cities we already know and could call *tight* may assist us in doing that *tightening* from a human perspective.

The Super Tight project grew from a shared interest in very dense cities, particularly those in Asia. It also grew from anxieties about high urban density, which is noticeable in affluent, western cities; but also from the fact that the inhabitants of these cities in general now suffer more from the effects of isolation than from overcrowding. In the first decade of this century, the City of Melbourne was very successful at reconsolidating its metropolitan centre, and to a lesser extent its sprawling, radiating spokes. The consolidation was so successful that an influx of high-rise dwellings unleashed traditional anxieties about high density. These reactions were framed as a debate about urban planning regulations and the merits of European medium rise versus the delirious and intense verticality of Hong Kong.

Rather than analyse the quantifiable benefits, harms or risks of such development or policies, we asked: What are the qualities of cities that adapt to closeness, and could those adaptations continue without limit? Is there a more nuanced term that might describe the qualities found in very dense cities? How could those qualities be observed, imagined or designed? We curated a substantial exhibition titled Super Tight in 2019 and gathered contributors from Japan, Vietnam, China, Singapore and Korea. These contributors are designers in and observers of their cities; through their practices, they produced moving images of their cities and of their design works. In addition, they participated in a series of conversations held in the event space installations of the RMIT Design Hub Gallery in Melbourne.

This book is a reflection on that work and on the ideas that emanated from it, particularly from the perspective of architecture and urbanism. It aims to establish and discuss a visual vocabulary for urban life built on intense closeness. However well understood the pressing need to consolidate cities might be, imagining this compaction as real and desirable is essential. This work places emphasis on the knowledge embodied in the image, and in the informal dialogue. Since the time of that exhibition and its many conversations, our cities have endured a pandemic that has recast nearly everything in urban life. Paradoxically, the notion of living closer together suddenly seemed absurd to consider, at least for a moment, yet those circumstances have also brought all the questions of tightness as a spatial and social concept into brutally sharp focus.

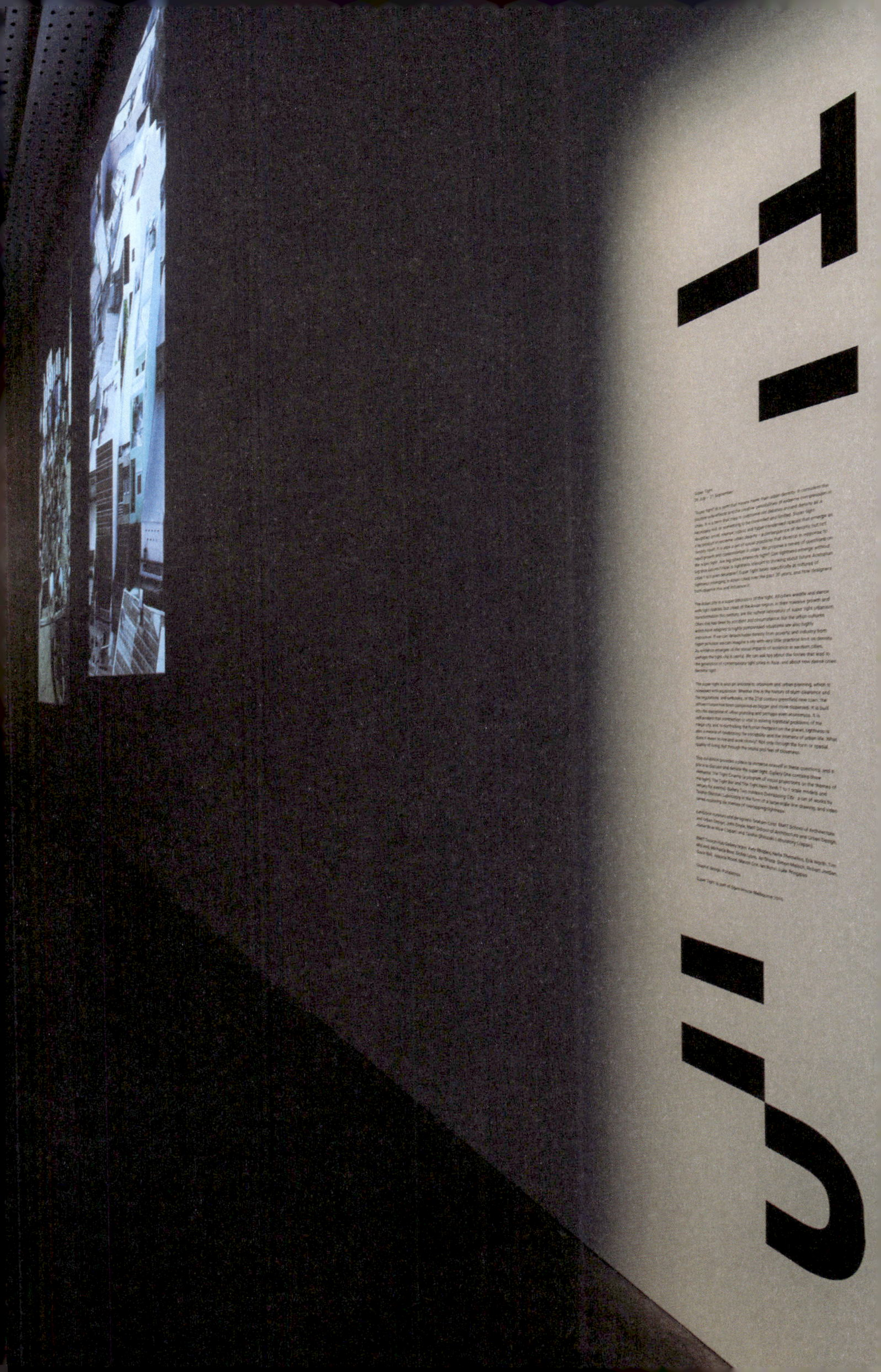

Reflections on Tightness After COVID

From a conversation with Yoshiharu Tsukamoto in September 2021

In conditions of extreme density, people can ignore conventional solutions and invent something new. It creates a chance for people to rethink or question the ordinary. To ask, what is usual or common? It also provides a chance to design unexpected hybrids. The dense urban condition, therefore, makes us question and invent today's livelihood.

Tightness is not only about size: it is about the relationship between things. For example, when we work with a skilful contractor for many projects, we say, 'the relationship is quite *tight* between the architect and the contractor.' So, *tightness* is more about relationships. In a dense urban environment, surrounded by small scale buildings, we are often very restricted in space. We might describe this as a *tight* relationship. *Tightness* is the key to architectural detail. To design architecture that stimulates the senses, you need a careful understanding of how many things can exist in the same place. This is also an issue of *tightness.*

During the pandemic, we have been surrounded by an invisible wall that limits our capacity to move around the city. Staying at home during the lockdowns hasn't been a positive experience for many of us. Perhaps one positive thing from this period is that we now cook a lot more! Although the Tokyo government is yet to adopt the idea of a fifteen-minute walkable city, unlike Paris, Barcelona or Shanghai, it is still very easy to walk around the old area of Tokyo. There are many services still within the residential fabric, which transform these areas of the city into more walkable neighbourhoods. The idea of the walkable city is another type of *tightness,* where the house could have small services for others to share.

The interior of the house contains certain behaviours that relate to *tightness*. For example, until the beginning of the Showa period, people slept and ate in a tatami room. In the tatami room – you can change the mode of use by changing the devices. For instance, the table used for dining is foldable. After dinner, you pack it up and bring the futon from the cupboard and turn this room into a sleeping space and fold the futon down and put it back in the cupboard. This behaviour allows us to use one room for several purposes. Even in a farmhouse, where the room for sleeping is fixed, they prepare a futon before sleep and put it into storage again in the morning. This behaviour is not because of smallness: it works well in smallness, but it is not a consequence of smallness.

It is interesting to revisit the transformation of the single-family house, first introduced to Japan in the 1920s. In the course of the 20th Century, the house became more and more designed and oriented towards a nuclear family. It became introverted and extremely small. We need to understand the premises that shaped these changes. Understanding it helps to find new ways for the house to be occupied. Atelier Bow-Wow recently designed a house with one giant room with tiny rooms attached and without a fence around the property. The giant room can adapt to communal activities and the tiny rooms serve for sleeping and bathing. The contrast challenges the single-family house by examining the assumptions of suburban residential development. The pandemic has opened various opportunities to think about this.

The single-family house highlights issues of property ownership. In Japan, houses are detached from neighbouring buildings in order to make ownership clear. Atelier Bow-Wow is currently working with two sisters who inherited the house built by their father. The property has already been divided into two, but the house is still on the lot, violating the new boundary division. The building is still in good shape, but it is difficult to keep it and fit their requests, including future saleability as an independent piece of land.

Projects like this make us confront issues of finance, property ownership, and the tax system. It's not easy to change, but architects must challenge these rhetorics. This social context has favoured individualism and the single-family detached house and has reinforced the gender divisions. The pandemic has revealed that architecture is responsible for these issues. We've discovered that shared living and establishing commons are expected to reduce the impact on the environment. Hopefully, this trend will continue to develop further, even after the pandemic ends.

The pandemic has also made people think of moving to farming areas. I'm working in Kamogawa, Chiba prefecture, which is a one and half hour drive from Tokyo. Every weekend, I bring students to work together with two migrant colleagues. One of them is an artist and a farmer, and the other is a permaculturalist. We three established an association called "Small Earth" to revitalise a farming village that is confronting population decline and deterioration. In this project, I met interesting *satoyama* migrants from Tokyo that moved to establish new ways of living.

They grow vegetables, rice and practice forestry and produce burning charcoal. They work collectively for the construction of houses. Some are good at mud wall rendering, others good at woodwork, thatched roofs etc. They teach and learn from each other to reach what I call *Migrant Vernacular.* They have even established a local currency. This convivial way of living is attracting many people. I have met architects, editors, professors and TV producers, all of whom had previously lived and worked in Tokyo.

So, living and working in rural settings is becoming a real option for urban residents. The relationship between the two areas has further room to develop. The land that is being transformed into suburban areas outside Tokyo was previously farmland or forest. In some areas, farming activity is still taking place, but mostly the farming activity has disappeared and the land has been transformed into sites for construction. The farming village I visit each weekend hasn't had good accessibility until the Aqua-Line under sea tunnel opened. Now it takes 1.5 hours to travel from Tokyo. Suddenly these rural areas have become quite accessible for urban residents.

Work is a central factor in rethinking our livelihood. Many people admire life in a rural environment but hesitate to move there because it's hard to find work. If you have children, the school system is another barrier for a family to move from the city to a farming area. To overcome these barriers, remote working and school exchange programs can allow families to bring their life into a rural setting. Then you would be involved in farming. This hybrid lifestyle is still rare but a convincing model for the future.

Ownership is also an issue even in rural areas. On the Bōsō Peninsula, rent for rural properties is very low, and many farms are abandoned and require maintenance, which means some landowners are willing to allow groups to work the land for very lower rents. *Satoyama* culture, for example, values prosperity without growth instead of sustainable development. It's challenging to stop or limit growth in these settings, which is consequence of rich networks of things from the place.

In the same context, one old house in the centre of the village recently went on sale. My local colleague tried to find someone in his network to buy this property, but it's very difficult to for people to maintain a farm, a house and a mountain.

Finally, we decided to buy it collectively. So around thirty people purchased a share in this house. Of course, this is still ownership, but it is collective. Collective ownership is a strategy for preserving heritage buildings. We often joke that we have one foot in capitalism and the other foot outside of it. This expression, borrowed from Anna Tsing's book *The Mushroom at the End of the World* describes the edge of capitalism through her experiences foraging for rare mushrooms.

Perhaps we can understand the term *super tight* through networks rather than space. So much of the critical language in architecture and urbanism that appeared in the twentieth century was governed by the term *space*. It is challenging to discuss architecture now without using this magic term. Space externalises networks; it has emancipated us from the old networks. But space can't fully explain the networks which support today's cities and livelihoods. It is the key to understanding the deterioration of the planet or the divide between south and the north. Having more space detaches us from our networks. Understanding urban networks might change our view of urban *tightness*. It might value connection and networks over the freedoms or separation of space. This is an issue to keep discussing for the future.

01

A conversation with Yoshiharu Tsukamoto, Nigel Bertram and Anna Jankovic

John: Melbourne is a really *loose* city – most of it is very low density. How do we design *tightly* in such a *loose* city?

Tsukamoto: There is value in *looseness*. People appreciate it; the question is how to make a city dense while keeping that *looseness*. It's important to introduce a gradual process, rather than drastic densification. Tokyo became denser and denser, but it took almost 70 years to achieve this condition. In the beginning, it wasn't so *tight*. Properties were gradually subdivided into smaller pieces. This change was happening slowly: people had enough time to adapt and create a comfortable living environment. Tokyo's density is based on detached two or three storey high housing, all very close to one another. Many of them are wooden construction, so it's still very accessible – anyone can intervene. This *looseness* allows people to customise the density into something comfortable.

Anna: Yes, Tokyo isn't the densest city, but it does have certain *tightness*. Can that be designed as we approach increased density? Melbourne doesn't have mechanisms like inheritance tax, where land plots divide like cells. Melbourne tends to densify with drastic shifts in building scale.

Tsukamoto: In Tokyo, we also have special districts designated as urban regeneration centres. It's a government initiative to upgrade parts of the city to attract foreign investors.

Nigel: Melbourne has a native *tight* and *loose* environment – the inner suburbs, terrace house fabric. For instance, these areas are *looser* now than they once were in terms of population density. But the way people live in these neighbourhoods is very creative – retrofitting current social dynamics within the previous physical fabric. The challenge is to build new environments that have this quality and to renovate the less *tight* suburbs of the middle ring. This kind of careful retrofitting is crucial.

John: We talk about *tightness* as a negotiated by-product: it isn't curated by city government or developers. Is it possible to design *tightness* from the beginning? Can we curate it ourselves?

Tsukamoto: I think we can plan cities with qualities of *tightness* from the beginning. We can learn from what we have experienced in Tokyo.

Nigel: One consideration could be social *tightness*. Social *tightness* is really distinct from density. It involves sharing and an awareness of a neighbour or other people around you. One thing that stops *tightness* from occurring in our city is overlooking laws that say "you shall not see any of your neighbours' activities" – we must have our own complete internalised world within our property. *Tight* environments are where people's social life and their ownership overlap. This means that ownership doesn't completely encapsulate the life we live. It does happen, but it's being regulated out and that regulatory framework is limiting. Behaviour is super important here. One of the big cultural differences is how people behave in physical proximity to each other. People in Japan are better at modifying their own behaviour to deal with the presence of others whereas, our de-facto suburban mentality means that we don't have to modify our behaviour. We can do whatever we like inside our property.

Anna: Within the fenced confines...

Nigel: Yes, behind the fence. You should be able to yell and scream, light fires and burn something down or fix your car. Not modifying our behaviour is the default position. The difficulty as we densify is learning how to modify behaviour in a relevant, contemporary and Australian way.

Graham: How do we *tighten* the city without losing the value of looseness? The notion is that a denser city means more constrained behaviours, yet the thing that is valuable about the low-density Australian suburb is a certain freedom.

Nigel: Yes, and if you're worried about overlooking, put up a screen or close the curtain. If you're not worried about it, you do what you did in your house and look straight at the neighbour's window. It's about whether we're forced to or whether we can self-modify and self-adapt.

Graham: I've experienced a supreme example of this in Saigon. Such tolerance for a lack of privacy was new to me, I had an apartment where I could reach out of my bedroom window to the neighbour's kitchen. It's a condition that is very dense but super tolerant to a lack of privacy.

Nigel: Yes, and at a certain point of intensity, design becomes slightly irrelevant in an aesthetic sense. It becomes much more performative: it is about fitting everything in and feels less aesthetically controllable. The environments and behaviours that we've been talking about are successful because they let go of something to achieve that feeling of looseness. They have to let go of control over the neatness or the appearance of things in favour of their performance. That is one challenge for how designers might intervene in a performative rather than an aesthetic way.

John: So how do we set regulations that protect minimum levels of amenity without killing design?

Tsukamoto: I think the size of the building always matters. The biggest challenge today is that market efficiency always wants more space, more saleable floor area. This defines the business scope of the whole project, and it becomes a process of stacking saleable floorplates. Paris has been struggling with this for a long time. It has a very interesting approach to mixing private investors and social organisations in new developments. These are not new buildings; they are renovating and repurposing old buildings by sometimes adding two or three floors. The investor works together with the architects, and they have to provide specific types of social housing. It's a social program within a new housing project. So there are eight-storey building limits. They don't give housing to the real estate market, so there are fewer high-rise condominiums in Paris.

Anna: In Melbourne, the apartment living standards aren't just centred around the size of rooms or apartment *tightness*. It also refers to other good initiatives like access to light – things you may achieve in looser environments. But it is talking about a very high-density building typology. What we lack in Melbourne is the middle – what Nigel was referring to earlier. We have adaptive reuse sites in our inner-city suburbs but quite large towers in the city centre. We're missing the middle scale, the four to eight-storey type is something our suburbs are equipped to adopt, but the opportunities haven't presented themselves.

Nigel: The market doesn't seem to be able to take up that scale for a range of reasons. On the regulatory question, what you were describing in Paris sounds like a negotiated complex outcome, which is a result of a discussion between parties all with different criteria. Regulations like height limits or setbacks are very blunt instruments to make a city. It's not guaranteed, even if you comply with these rules, that the outcome will be good. In Melbourne, the examples that work are where people sit down and negotiate their own kind of performance criteria: the cooperative housing models where people get together and say, 'We've got a shared mutual interest. What are we going to decide on?' We are aware of body corporate structures where you can get thirty owners together to agree to do something. Often they're dysfunctional relationships, but they can have positive outcomes by working collectively on mutual self-interests. Those kinds of negotiated performance-based outcomes are much more powerful than any regulation, whether it's size or height or volume. There are ethnographic studies that prove that the ideal size of group for these sorts of negotiations is around thirty. Beyond that figure, people naturally split off into groups. This number is used by co-housing groups and organisations. They've studied this to work out when a group becomes dysfunctionally large.

John: That conveniently makes three or four floors on a 500 square metre site – a minimum unit of urbanism.

Nigel: That would be a good regulation: do anything you like but only in groups of thirty.

Graham: Bringing the discussion back to Tokyo: one by-product of post-war redistribution was to create a huge number of small size landowners. The tendency here, and the tendency of the market, fully supported by planning policies, is to consolidate bigger and bigger chunks of land to create bigger projects in one hit. That works against the very distributed land ownership that you might see in Tokyo.

Tsukamoto: In Tokyo, it is very difficult to do. But Mori, a famous Tokyo developer, took twenty years to collect small properties in Roppongi. It then took eight years to build the skyscrapers.

Graham: We have a highly atomised ownership in Australia. The average owner is stuck to the limits of their block. But there is a trend where adjacent neighbours are beginning to realise that their properties are worth more together than separately. So they might take some risks together.

Nigel: If you can share the risk in smaller chunks, more like the 30 than the 3000, then this middle scale might have ways of appearing. People are trying to do this like the Baugruppen or the work of Geoffrey London. They are trying to find processes where neighbours can collaborate, share risk and be their own developers. So that is a cooperative negotiated outcome. It might encourage outcomes that are more likely to result in tightness.The owner of a single suburban lot is stuck both ways. They can't consolidate, but it's also difficult to subdivide. One thing preventing the density of cities like Melbourne, apart from the core, is the difficulty of subdividing and making smaller lots. Two neighbours could get together and join their lot, or one person could cut it in half and give it to two different people – both have an advantage.

Graham: Dual occupancy all over the city is exactly this process. Yet the way it is done in Melbourne is typically a negative outcome – trees are chopped down, and an ill-considered building is dumped behind the other building. In Tokyo, it is that same process, but it is a kind of market-led vernacular.

Nigel: Maybe we're partway through a process that happened very clearly in Tokyo. Generations of housing are mixed up in interesting ways, whereas it feels like our suburbs are now being subdivided for the first time after fifty years. So it took fifty years of stasis to get enough pressure for the second generation of houses to be built. What would a second and third generation of the suburbs look like?

Anna: Perhaps the multi-generational home offers a clue. Houses can be designed to allow multiple generations of a family to live on the same site without moving or redeveloping. Maybe the house typology itself is going to have to change to account for each generation living in the same area.

Nigel: Yes, the richness and diversity of household structure is where all are present together; not one replacing the other. It's like a farm where you just keep adding one shed to the first.

Graham: We should remember that the average house size in Australia has doubled since the 1980s. Small suburban houses on big lots used to be common, then they grew. They peaked a few years ago and are now getting smaller again. There is familiarity amongst older people of much smaller houses even in this country.

Anna: The impact of cars is another example. Negotiation also works at a larger scale, perhaps at a policy level with municipal governments. An example of this issue is the car parking in the Nightingale projects. They had to fight the planning authorities to have no car parking in several of their projects. Now its policy in many local councils and other councils are starting to consider this change. It took a profound challenge to question the necessity of the car.

Tsukamoto: I convinced several clients to give up having a car because their property was too small and they had a limited budget. Why do you spend money and space on a garage? It's better to use this space for human beings. If they don't accept that, it's difficult to design a townhouse in Tokyo.

Anna: Living in close proximity to others is often seen as a negative thing. It has pejorative connotations with poverty and even crime. As architects, we have a responsibility to communicate the value of spaces. These can be small, *tight* or *loose* while also communicating that having less isn't necessarily a negative. We are witnessing a cultural shift – people are not necessarily associating ownership of objects as denoting wealth.

Nigel: Housing is perhaps one of the hardest things to adjust – for obvious reasons. So much capital is tied up in the house. It's like forcing the consumer to handle the recycling problem. So much of the excess of the city is all the stuff outside of the house, whether it be public space or poorly distributed retail.

Graham: The public space of Melbourne laneway bar culture is an example of *tightness*. Melbourne accidentally became really good at that, and it happened through a series of regulatory and economic circumstances and demonstration projects like Six Degrees' *Meyers Place* bar. So through this demonstration project, a culture evolved. The creativity that allowed that to erupt in the city in what previously was a space for rubbish collection could happen in other environments and settings.

Nigel: It's a great example that is entirely voluntary: people actively choose and desire to go into those incredibly *tight* spaces. No one is forcing you to go in.

Anna: These are postcard moments Melbourne, but somehow these qualities haven't translated to the home context.

Tsukamoto: Ultimately, as architects, the key to understanding the potential of these spaces and the behaviours in the city is drawing and observing in a careful manner. I think that brings you another dimension of understanding. That is the evidence: the proof that things can change in the future.

02

Overlapping and Sharing in Tight Cities

with Taishin Shiozaki

The overlapping of functions in physical space is critical to the *tight* use of cities and adaptations to density. Far from being functionally segregated or zoned, sharing space for multiple, simultaneous events produces both the pleasures and the efficiencies of *tightness*.

Very dense environments are often imagined obsessively through a quantified or measured formula. The image of a very dense utopia is formal fields of tightly condensed elements. Michael Wolf's photo series *The Architecture of Density* captures this condition in Hong Kong's ubiquitous housing estates.[1] This density is an intricate formal network extending to micro-apartments and other compartmentalised and unitised components. It is a system where the functions of living in tiny spaces are regulated through modules of functional separation.

In fact, *tight* cities require a high degree of organisational and functional *looseness* to operate. As density increases, it becomes necessary to set aside the separation of functions in daily life. When space is limited, arbitrarily designating only one activity to a location is not a legitimate luxury. The tendency to compartmentalise functions within an architectural plan is driven by social expectations and status.

The concept of overlapping in architecture and urbanism describes a condition in which space and its functions are collapsed. Rather than allocating a distinct space for each activity, a single space becomes the backdrop to the ever-changing series of occupations. Observations of public space in Japan show how spaces play host to a broad number of activities that can vary from extremely dense to completely empty depending on daily, weekly and annual cycles.[2] Similar observations can be made about a building's interior. Rather than being simply small, a *tight* space can be multi-functional, multi-generational, multi-household containers where all aspects of life might play out.

If this logic is amplified for the design of future architectures and cities, it would result in a dramatic reduction in the physical and environmental footprint of settlements. Though self-evident, it flies in the face of more than a hundred years of urban planning orthodoxy. The legacy of architecture and urban planning in the twentieth century has been a resistance to density, but also a restraint on the use of spaces independent of their design intent.

Despite substantial revisions to modern functionalist planning in the twenty-first century, the paradigm which defined the previous century has remained pervasive.

The organisation of the built environment along functional lines has become so axiomatic that we forget how recently it was adopted or that cities and architecture existed and flourished for thousands of years before its dominance.

The great urban planning projects that emerged in the nineteenth century all share consistent themes. The Garden City movement initiated by Ebenezer Howard in the 1890s, for instance, sought to depopulate a city that was viewed as overcrowded and unhealthy. The city would be reorganised with residential and living spaces separated from industry, just as the healthy were separated from the clinic or asylum. Green belts of agriculture and parkland act as buffers between functions. A similar impulse to separate the residents is present in CIAM's work of the 1930s.

'CIAM demanded that housing districts should occupy the best sites, and… buildings should not be built along transportation routes, and modern techniques should be used to construct high apartment building spaces widely apart, to free the soil for large green parks.'[3]

Such urban manifestos prevailed and became hugely influential during the urban reconstruction after the Second World War. Much of the urban form and the orthodoxies of urban planning are predicated on a version of these principles, even if the implementation or the rhetoric has gradually evolved. The specific public health concerns of the early industrial city were barely relevant by the time these approaches were adopted as policy and even less relevant today. However, the notion of mono-functional zoning persists.

As previously mentioned, the functionalist movements in urban design and planning were accompanied by similar approaches to architectural planning and organisation. An early expression of programmatic functionalism in architecture was evident following world war one in Germany; *Article 155* of the Weimar Constitution mandated the provision of a 'healthy dwelling' for all citizens. This term drove the exploration of new models of housing to address a national shortage. In particular, the development of models organised around what came to be known as *Existenzminimum,* or subsistence dwelling, dominated architectural discourse in Germany. This attitude was prominent in the newly-formed Bauhaus but later throughout Europe. The second CIAM conference in 1929 focused on the exploration of the minimum dwelling and the optimisation of functional relationships within it.

'The running of a home consists of precise functions in a regular order. The regular order of these functions constitutes a phenomenon of circulation. An exact, economic rapid circulation is the key to contemporary architecture. The precise functions of domestic life require various areas whose minimum content can be quite precisely determined. For each function there must be a type of minimum "container," standard, necessary, and sufficient (the human scale). The order of these functions is established according to a logic which is biological, and not geometrical. These functions can be diagrammed along a continuous line; whereupon the interplay of the necessary areas and their proximities can be clearly discerned.'[4]

The space of the house should be set out for specific functions within a clearly demarcated sequence, precluding contingency, uncertainty and adaptation. Mapping the patterns of shared or overlapping use begins to unravel the certainty of functionalist modernism. As cities were reconstructed, the functionalist minimum dwelling became an organising unit. But the need for a minimum of healthy dwelling fell away, the functionalist residential diagram has remained. Today, the ubiquitous volume houses at the fringes of most cities pervert the minimum set of domestic functions – expanding it to include rumpus rooms, pool rooms, walk-in robes, single-use spaces made for the marketing and consumption of function. They also exclude the random public work of public spaces.

'There are two types of cities, cities where you can weld on the sidewalk and cities where you can't.'[5]

It is possible to design for *tightness,* but the history of the last century suggests it is more successful when it develops organically, like a piece of work on the sidewalk. It has often emerged as a by-product of rapid urbanisation, including in informal settlements. Explosive urban growth in the late twentieth century, particularly in the global south, drew on western models of city planning but at a pace that outstripped its ability to enforce and control density. Planning controls for rapidly urbanising environments are often loose, broad or, in the case of informal settlements, non-existent.

Informal settlements usually exhibit spatial compression and high population density, but one of the key by-products of their loose planning regime is a free-wheeling functional mix. Free from the obligation to organise and separate activities, spaces are located wherever most convenient or practical. When contemporary planning celebrates functional diversity, it does it within limits of scale, density and propriety.

Ian Lambot
Kowloon Walled City
Hong Kong

Matthaus Wander
Chungking Mansion
Hong Kong

The infamous Kowloon Walled City in Hong Kong grew to become the most densely settled place on earth. By the 1990s, when it was demolished, it housed more than 50,000 people in 2.6 hectares. By comparison Mong Kok, the densest district of Hong Kong currently houses around 1,300 people per hectare – 14 times less dense than the Walled City. The legacy of that settlement divides town planners and architects. Regarded as a work of unbelievable formal and sectional intricacy, at the same time, it is used as a cautionary demonstration of the necessity of city planning controls. Sitting outside the rule of municipal governance, it was allowed to densify beyond accepted norms. More significantly, the organic generation of its form and the extreme spatial constraints resulted in the total mixture and integration of functions. Within a compressed footprint equivalent to a typical city block, all living, eating, commerce, industry, sanitation and leisure occurred in a regime of total overlapping land use. Setting aside the deep socio-economic problems of the settlement, the Walled City suggests that extremes of urban density can only be negotiated through the dissolution of segregation and by sharing and overlapping space.

Other examples of intensely mixed-use compound buildings persist in Hong Kong. Chungking Mansions, an aggregate of several 17 storey towers, were intended as residential apartments but now house a mixture of small hotels, hostels, offices, shops, salons, clinics, restaurants, bars, workshops, and import and export traders. The complex has a large residential population, both transient and permanent. It is also a mercantile hub, including a huge volume of mobile phone sales. Although it does not match the density of the Kowloon Walled City, it is frequently compared to the earlier settlement. As a result, it is loosely regulated by the Hong Kong government.[6] The interior of the compound has been intensely subdivided. What was intended as apartments have been divided into multi-room guest houses. Others have become shops located far above street level. Workshops that in many cities are positioned at the urban periphery sit alongside offices that organise for the sale and transport of goods globally. Chungking Mansion is one of many compound buildings in the city that perform in a similar manner.

Is it possible for urban planning to catch up with rapid growth and take on a greater role in shaping the direction of the city? Or do cities naturally ossify, becoming more functionally segregated, and controlling density through traditional planning models? Before the advent of the automobile in Tokyo, there was no difference between footpaths and driveways; it was easy to find mixing and overlapping in streets crowded with varied activities.

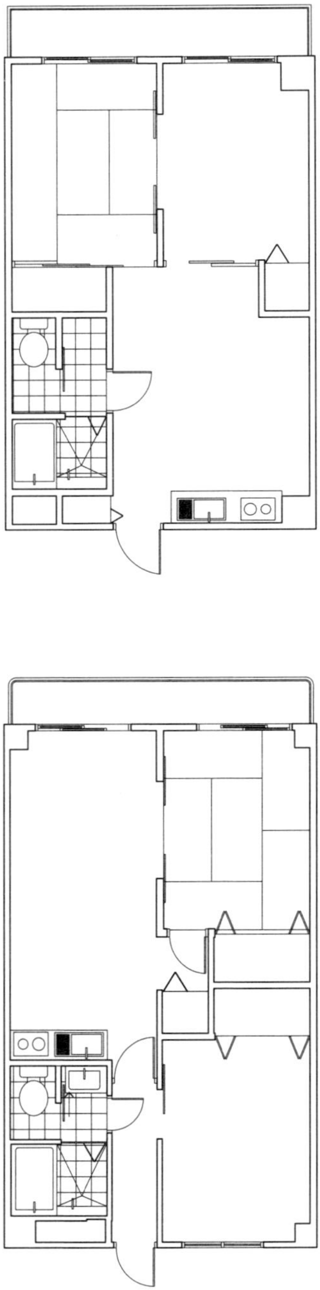

Typical 2LDK
Apartment Plans

By 1945, many cities in Japan had been completely destroyed by war. Governments directed urban planning toward post-war reconstruction. Kenzo Tange's master plan was vital to the future of the country. Using axes and cores, Tange created the basic structure of the city from the position of *tabula rasa*. The realisation of Metabolist projects occurred in a context of high economic growth. The core and capsule forms have now become symbols of urban density. During Japan's bubble economy of the 1980s and 1990s, desire and consumption accelerated extreme urban densification. The functional division of space and use was replaced by a seemingly random commercial density driven by capital.

This extreme form of urban growth and densification was particular to Japanese cities. Yet all cities have cycles of urban consolidation caused by economic surges as well as human intimacy caused by lifestyles and cultures overlapping and coexisting. For housing, the functional division of spaces has survived since modernism. In Japan, for example, houses are described by the shorthand of nLDK. That is living, dining and kitchen, where *n* is the number of private bedrooms. A large, 4-bedroom dwelling can be described as a 4SLDK with the additional S indicating an extra spare room such as a storage or study beyond the four bedrooms. This pure functional notation of rooms and purposes has emerged as a departure from the traditional Japanese floor plan, where various uses overlap and are not designated.

While the LDK idea is conventional in Japan, it was revolutionary in western countries. To fold the three activities of cooking, eating and leisure into a single undefined space was novel in volume housing until recently. The common expectation was that each function would have its enclosed zone within the house, regardless of use patterns. With the expansion of apartment living in Australian cities, the gradual integration of these functions into the open plan has not only compressed the footprint but resulted in the adoption of the LDK model. Spatial sharing and overlapping is an endpoint to this process, but also its beginning. Functional separation is often described through utility, yet the greatest state of utility is one that transcends functional specificity.

The shed type is perhaps the prime example of architecture that overlaps and shares space. Sheds come in many shapes and sizes but are rarely associated with density. As a model, they have the potential to be considered *tight* through their functional indifference. These structures are typically a large, free span, loose envelope. Their use is limited only by the scale and proportion of this envelope, the interior is free to be used flexibly. Modest examples include pre-fabricated utilitarian garages, workshops or greenhouses.

Graham Crist
2J House
Toodyay

Baracco Wright
Garden House
Western Port Bay

ODDO Architects
CH House
Hanoi

A comparison can be made with the flexible large span containers of the modernist era, a tradition that continues in the contemporary work of Lacaton & Vassal and Barracco Wright and Antarctica Architects in Australia.

Vietnam's *tube houses* are associated with formal *tightness* and are often located in very densely populated urban *hẻms*.[7] These types are very narrow, tall towers, common to urban conditions with compressed street frontages; they are a peculiarity of Vietnamese urban character. Coupled with a very *tight* physical footprint is an extremely diverse range of activities accommodating a loose urban and household arrangement. The *hẻms* also host a diverse range of overlapping activities, social community space, commerce, a de facto civic realm and domestic sphere are unusually blurred through the 24-hr cycle. The lower levels of many *tube houses* are effectively commercial spaces operating from domestic dwellings – blurring both the private living space and the street outside. It is an extreme shophouse. Traditionally, these buildings are occupied by a large household of extended families or multiple families.

The *CH House* (2019) in Hanoi by ODDO Architects also integrates a multi-generational household and commercial space within a single *tight* building. The commercial shop front and café occupy the lower two levels. The domestic living spaces, including the kitchen, dining and lounge areas, operate as the transition and intermediary between the commercial space below and the sleeping quarters above. The house accommodates a family of young children, their parents, and grandparents. While the dwelling is large by Vietnamese standards, it is narrow – 4.5m wide and 35 metres in length. A large portion of the dwelling is taken up by circulation. The design provides for a series of discrete sleeping and bathing areas, though the remainder of the spaces within the dwelling form continuous living spaces split across levels. Certain areas are functionally specific, such as the kitchen, yet the majority of the network of open living spaces within the dwelling are ambiguous in their functional designation. This allows for spaces to be inhabited opportunistically by groups within the family at different times of the day and for many purposes. Likewise, the commercial space below can serve as overflow living space by simply opening the door and allowing access up and down the staircases. By placing the access point to the dwelling through the shopfront, there is a continuous micro-process of negotiation and overlap of function between commercial and residential occupants.

Atelier Bow-Wow
House & Atelier
Tokyo

Atelierco
Kikuna Pit House
Kanagawa

Atelierco
Kikuna Pit House
Kanagawa

In Japan, the emergence of micro-allotments and tiny footprints has triggered the creation of a detached housing type with an extremely open and fluid section. The houses of Atelier Bow-Wow frequently use a series of open platforms that allow for functional specificity while permitting spatial openness within the house interior. House and Atelier (2005) combines Atelier Bow-Wow's office and the living quarters of the company's directors within a single continuous vertical volume organised around a staggered stair and platforms.

Similarly, the Pithouse in Kikuna designed by Atelierco (Saeco Kobayashi and Taishin Shiozaki) illustrates a hyper fluid building section within a single open volume. The project is a renovated wooden house located in the hills of Yokohama. Originally built as a sharehouse for students, it was sold three years ago to teachers. The most common type of house built on sloping land in outside of Tokyo is a reinforced concrete platform serving as a parking space and supporting a wooden frame over it with no relationship to that platform. The original sharehouse for students did not require a parking space, so there was a large area lying under the floor unoccupied. This allowed the creation of a one-room house where the wooden structure opens down to the structural floor below. On this site, various uses spatially and temporally overlap. There is a clear connection from the upper level of the house, which has a view to Mt Fuji, to the structural floor that covers archaeological remains dating back thousands of years. The current owners are teachers who frequently use the house as a location for teaching seminars. So, who is the house designed for? What is its functional designation? One room plays host to living and teaching. It expands in sections as trees sprout through the foundations to grow into the space above. By interlacing various scales and periods of occupation, the concept of fixed ownership is liberated.

Architecture in the tropics, either vernacular or twentieth-century modernism, isn't always associated with *tight* density. Hot and humid urban environments demand openness in form, material, and spatial planning. It is precisely this loose fit approach to functional planning and the volume which facilitates overlapping use. A housing type built into a cultural vernacular and driven by climate can intensify use through its loosened functional definition.

Kampung Admiralty
WOHA
Singapore

Kampung Admiralty
WOHA
Singapore

Hotel Pickering
WOHA
Singapore

A recent example of this model is the Kampung Admiralty housing designed by Singapore office WOHA. The project was developed through the Singapore Housing and Development Board, which accounts for around 80% of the city's housing. It includes 104 units ostensibly configured for senior citizens. The complex is loosely modelled on the Malay *kampung,* a village unit that is self-contained and partially self-governing. Like its predecessor, Kampung Admiralty is intended to be self-contained with a broad mixture of functions arranged within a vertical campus. The project was established to support senior citizens to age in place within higher density well-connected neighbourhoods. The programmatic mixture supports this through the inclusion of essential healthcare, childcare and education facilities, in addition to the usual mix of retail and entertainment.

The unique aspect of this project, in a city as dense and expensive as Singapore, is the commitment to providing unprogrammed space. Housing units, tenancies, and vertical circulation are carefully controlled but interspersed by a network of open spaces that are functionally ambiguous. These include terrace gardens and hard landscaping that is both covered and open. What these spaces offer is the possibility of multiple unplanned events taking place within a single space – an affordance of overlapping or creating gaps in function. A video WOHA made of the project (2019) shows the ground floor plaza operating as the access point, a meeting point for residents, a place to do dance and aerobics classes, and a dining hall for the building. All of this occurs without demarcation and within the same space.

If we consider *tightness* as an adaptation to density, it is a kind of social efficiency which leads to a smaller physical footprint. There is an efficiency and *tightness* to overlapping the use of space for many functions and events. This quality is evident in designed and observed projects and in the unplanned use of urban spaces in daily life. Yet, the impulse to compartmentalise function remains part of the logic of modern spatial planning. No spaces are entirely indeterminate functionally, and all have the capacity for unintended occupation. *Super tight* architecture foregrounds this value; it juggles circumstance and need and proposes that being functionally open-ended and loosely determined is of greatest utility. That loose, ad-hoc utility leads to a *tighter* urban footprint.

03

An interview with Professor Tohru Horiguchi from Kindai University, Osaka

Graham: Let's examine your take on the theme of the *supertight*, in particular the video made in the *Bingo House* bar.

Tohru: There are several phenomena and places that we are interested in documenting. For this film, we focused on a standing bar in Japan that has been there for quite a long time. We found that there is something different in how people behave and the way people occupy the place. We call it *Bingo House*, not after bingo the game but after a specific liquor shop. It is located somewhere between Osaka and Hiroshima.

Graham: Would you consider the bar unusual in the Japanese context, or would you see it as quite a typical way of setting up a bar?

Tohru: People prefer to go to a standing bar instead of a place to sit down. At the *Bingo House*, I was first interested in standing bars with a counter. I was interested in people's distance. It's not fixed, if it's crowded, you have to squeeze in, and if it's not, it will be *loose*. I was looking for this type of space, and my graduate students showed me Bingo House. They don't have a counter: they have smaller segments of tables that are self-served. I had never seen this in Japan before. At the entrance, you are given your table number. If it's crowded, you have to share that small table. There is a counter and staff at the bar – one person is in charge of beer, another the sake, one for the food and another for dry snacks.

Graham: So, you just take it from the counter and pay at the end?

Tohru: Yes. The way people stand around the small table is also interesting, but the space against the wall also gets busy.

Graham: Presumably, the way people interact in this space is critical.

Tohru: The bar is right next to a busy train station, the largest station in Osaka. They open from early evening or late afternoon, and they close at either 8:00pm or 9:00pm, quite early.

Graham: I'm thinking about how people interact, particularly with strangers here, and this conversation about the type being a particular density. It might have a lot to do with social behaviours and learning how to occupy space in a particular way.

Tohru: Yes, we have had more and more inbound tourists since 2015, and we're expecting this will get higher closer to the Olympics. This increase in foreign travel will change the social mix – instead of sharing time and space with people of the same homogeneous background.

Graham: So you're suggesting that the ability to interact very closely in Japanese cities is to do with a homogenous population?

Tohru: Maybe. The standing bars we see today are the third or fourth generation. The first of these bars started with sake and liquor shops which opened during the day and then in the evening you could drink in the shop. Fifteen or twenty years ago, there was a tapas bar trend which was often in an old space and appealed to a mixed crowd of young people. But *Bingo House* is mainly Japanese. Other types of standing bars have more and more foreign guests, especially the new fusion types.

Graham: There are plenty of standing bars in Europe – standing around drinking is a very British thing to do. The particular bar you filmed has tables like a restaurant, which is strange. It is a hybrid of a sitting and a standing bar.

Tohru: I agree that the standing bar style is more common in western culture. Serving sushi started in standing bars. Now it is high-end food, but it used to be fast food. It is cheap, and most Japanese don't stay long in standing bars.

John: Is this the first time you've made films in your lab?

Tohru: Yes, this was the first time I used a film as research. Maybe I will continue.

Graham: There is something about the component of time, which reshapes how you think about space. There is a sense that people are coming, going and moving around – the *tightness* is different to a still shot of an empty bar or an architectural drawing of it at full capacity. The film captures the capacity to occupy a place intensely through people coming and going frequently.

Tohru: We deliberately didn't edit or change the time or speed in the film. We simply connected the scenes.

Graham: It struck me that architects often think like engineers. They think about the worst case, so for instance, you design to maximum capacity. But you're rarely at that maximum capacity, and a space is more comfortable at a higher density than you think.

John: That idea is scalable. We often see road infrastructure scaled for maximum capacity, but it doesn't always meet that capacity.

Tohru: We couldn't capture the busiest time. We couldn't see the layout of the tables with all the people in the way.

Graham: In Japan, students work in laboratories or workshops; we've seen how close students get in those circumstances. What are your thoughts on the ingredients for a lively creative culture? Is it something about being close together, and overhearing each other's conversations, similar to being in the *Bingo House*?

Tohru: I don't know which bar they went to, but the Metabolist groups all went to the same place. They would go back to the same place again and again. There is a kind of incubation place, in specific bars, in the Golden Gai in Tokyo.

Graham: So they were regulars at one or two of them?

Tohru: I think there are some bars where actors or filmmakers still bartend once a week or fairly regularly. It's like a cultural time capsule.

Graham: I'm wondering what people do after leaving the standing bar in Osaka. What kind of home or neighbourhood are they going to? How far away? Lots of discussion around *tightness* is to do with housing. It is nice to think of this bar that you can go to for a short time and that it can be very, very *tight*. Are they likely to be travelling far from that bar when they leave?

Tohru: Most of them go to one or two more bars and then take the train home. They can commute for up to one hour or so. They either go to a suburban house or high-rise condominium next to a suburban station. That is based on the old train company's strategy – construct the line to the suburb and develop housing and a shopping mall around it. Employees of the company buy a home in these developments, commute to work and use the surrounding shopping centres. Tokyo and Osaka both have this same regional development model.

John: It is interesting that it is acceptable to have a conversation with someone in a small standing bar, but as soon as you step out, these expectations change, for instance on a train.

Graham: In a standing bar like this one, is it common to be alone and talk to a stranger across the table? Or are people mostly arriving in groups?

Tohru: At *Bingo House*, they come in smaller groups. If you go there alone, there is a counter for singles.

Graham: We're curious about this question of voluntarily seeking out *tightness* as opposed to it somehow being forced into it.

John: The most densely populated environments in Melbourne are probably bars. If the bar isn't full, people feel like they are in the wrong place. They will leave if it isn't happening. At the same time, people live in giant houses in the middle of nowhere and complain about the city getting too busy. Density is almost universally accepted in bars, but there is less tolerance for it in other settings.

Tohru: Many people in Japan have to commute by train. These are often unpleasant and overcrowded. Before getting on a train, we might have a drink in a small, overcrowded standing bar. In terms of personal space, these are similar experiences, and we don't avoid them. Ultimately, *tightness* is something that depends on the specifics of its context.

BEER
FOODS
GIFT
Liquor Shop
ビンゴヤ
ビンゴヤ
アサヒビール
MENU

04

Bingo House: A SuperTight Loose Standing Bar

Tohru Horiguchi

Bingo House is a standing bar located in central Osaka. It provides an interesting example of the *tight* inhabitation of a loosely arranged space. The bar contains no seats, just tables arranged around the space. It opens only for a few hours a day to cater to commuters, during which time it is intensely occupied.

BINGO-HOUSE is not a Bingo Hall.
BINGO-HOUSE is a shared platform of practicing spatio-temporal tightness emerged from the Japanese urban condition.

Bingo House is self service. Customers can take drinks as they like and pay at the end. Unlike other typical standing bars, *Bingo House* does not have a long bar counter. Instead, it has cut a longer bar counter into segments of small tables, distributing patrons and allowing for a more dense occupation.

The bar serves small dishes that customers pick up themselves. Tables are covered with plates at the end of the evening. *Bingo House* is located right next to a major train station, providing a stopover for workers on their commute back to home. The relationship between the density of its urban location, and its *loose* fit interior arrangement suggests a strategy for planning *tight* architecture.

05

A conversation with Minsuk Cho, Donald Bates, Emma Jackson, David Ma and Alban Mannisi

Minsuk: The video made for the *Super Tight* exhibition is titled *FREEZE!* and shows the building where we live and work. It was designed and built together with a few friends. The building was completed in August 2018, and we moved in right away. While we were thinking of showing some other projects for the *Super Tight* exhibition, we were skyping in front of the huge window in our office. The backdrop of the *tight* neighbourhood around us intrigued John and Graham. So we decided to include it in our contribution. The building exhibits the idea of *tightness* through the restrictions that limited its construction. It was planned to take thirteen months to build, but in the end, it took twenty. This was due to us having to negotiate every boundary with the neighbours. It was a social process. This neighbourhood, Itaewon, is probably the most multicultural area in Seoul.

John: We were intrigued by the view into your neighbour's property. Here in Melbourne, we have planning regulations that explicitly prohibit windows from looking into neighbouring properties. There is an urban gesture that is precipitated by opening up in that way. But this also comes with negotiating how the building is occupied.

Minsuk: A similar regulation was recently put in place in some districts in Korea. In our case, what you can see is just an old building next door. It is two metres away and has boilers and outdoor air conditioning units attached to the facade. These attachments were crossing over our property line, and we couldn't excavate unless we took them down. So we negotiated with the neighbour to leave them in place provided that they allow us to face our window towards them and use the surface of their building as a photo billboard. It was a win-win situation. But every boundary had to be negotiated with maybe five different neighbours because it is a complicated L-shaped lot. It has a lot of contact points – which also made it a nice way to meet the neighbours.

Graham: It's a nice description of the immediate environment. We've been discussing various cities and how they all seem to negotiate density slightly differently. Is there something about how this is filmed that says something particular about your environment?

Minsuk: Seoul is a very interesting city. More than 50 or 60 percent of the population is living in very dense conditions. However, most buildings are extremely small, not particularly tall, and separated by less than two metres. It's a really low but dense condition. The buildings are defined by one-metre setbacks from the boundary on both sides for fire evacuation. In most cases, nothing happens in these gaps.

Throughout the city, you see a lot of thriving, low-income neighbourhoods. Their success is in part due to this negotiation that takes place through architecture. Yet, many of these neighbourhoods are now in the process of being gentrified and becoming middle class. Hopefully, our move into the neighbourhood will not mean it becomes completely gentrified. I have seen that before and feel very guilty about it.

John: The mix of your building becomes clear through the film. It's not just the Mass Studies office – it's a mixed-use complex with a film production office.

Minsuk: My friend, a film director, along with his wife, an interior stylist, are also in the building. It's great to have her in the building as she collects nice furniture. There is another architect with about five people in her office. She is the curator and artistic director of the Korean Pavilion at the 2021 Venice Architecture Biennale. I'm happy to be in this kind of environment. This brings me back to the *super tight*. I think the difference between *tightness* and density is this social aspect; what it means to choose and define boundaries. There are almost 50 people working in this building which is more than 900m2 in floor area. Also, I am not a typical resident. I've never had a car in my life. I walk everywhere. Everything in my daily life, home and office, is within 12 minutes walk.

This is how I value the city – living compactly. The larger idea of *tightness* is about a compact city – it's also much more sustainable.

John: There is a different vision of what a walkable city looks like in Australia compared to cities like Seoul or Tokyo. I would consider Seoul to be incredibly walkable and a very well-organised city. Copenhagen is often used in these discussions. That is a city of less than a million, yet Greater Seoul is a megacity of around 25 million. But it doesn't feel that big when you're in it. Is it about shifting the image of a walkable city? Away from a village, into something really dense and capable of absorbing more contemporary population numbers.

Minsuk: The nature of the work we do requires a lot of travelling. But for most daily activities, we also stay within the neighbourhood. Coming back to Korea after living in New York and Holland for three years, where I cycled everywhere, I treat it as a little village. This is the only way to survive in Seoul because most people spend up to two hours a day commuting. I would rather just be lazy at home than commute, no matter how fancy and comfortable a car I could have.

Even though the greater Seoul area has more than 20 million people, the opposite of *tightness* has happened over the years. Seoul grew to 11 million in the late 1990s. Now, it's just below 10 million. Over the last 20 years, it shrunk. The population is ageing, but more importantly, it's sprawling because of neoliberal policies in real estate. People have been pushed further away from the centre of the city through market-driven price increases. I've also observed the depoliticisation of the city. The middle classes that are burdened with a mortgage, and other material expectations have become foot soldiers for the machine – soldiers for the Samsung empire. Somehow, things got stuck.

Graham: So the sprawling of the city or the dispersing of the city is a way of calming down or even dispersing political action or discontent?

Donald: If you look at where cities have sprawled, it's in countries that have an automobile industry. In Australia, before the Second World War and immediately after, most people used public transport. But Australia then decided it needed to be like America and have its own automobile industry. Then everything revolved around making it easy for the car, and it also produced a certain social and real estate model. The suburb and commute were okay because there were enough freeways to get quickly from point to point

Denmark never had an automobile industry. Another example is Paris. Our image of Paris mostly ignores its huge suburban enclaves and spread out conurbations. The same can be said about Rome and Milan. The automobile was seen as the primary industrial motive to generate wealth and jobs. It takes a lot of people to put together a single car, and you make just enough income to be able to buy one. It is then necessary to produce more cars. I agree that in the last 20 years, neoliberal real estate tendencies drove development. But it started back in the 1950s with the development of highway systems and automobile industries as the primary industrial moulder. Of course, these would prop up the oil industry. Between oil and automobiles, you have the basis of what we consider contemporary residential development.

Graham: What goes nicely with that automobile industry is the private property that you can easily buy. So at the end of that journey is a nice plot of land and a house to support your future wealth.

Donald: Boston in the early twentieth century developed suburbia based on tram and train lines. Before the automobile, public transport was often developed by private individuals. The same thing occurred in Melbourne: all the trams used to be private companies. They built the tram line to market property.

The tram companies saw the development of the tram line as an opportunity to develop and make money through real estate, yet it was simultaneously providing public transport. Since the mid-1950s, developers buy a piece of land and force the government to build the road to it. They only do the development part, not the infrastructure part.

David: Tokyo is a sprawling conurbation. Most of Tokyo is pretty much detached two-three storey housing. It puts a lot of small things together, but it's not necessarily a high-rise city.

John: What we are describing is the difference between density by numbers and density by a kind of socialisation. This also seems to be a constant theme of *Super Tight*.

Donald: There is a difference between using the word *tight* and the word dense. Dense seems to have a physical connotation. It talks about distances, certain proximities, how much can be put within a defined frame or volume. *Tight* goes back to what Minsuk was talking about – negotiation. For instance, when something is too *tight*, you have to decide to pull your elbows in. If you're standing on a busy tram or a train, you have to change your body to negotiate other proximities.

The term is different from the usual discourse on density or compact cities. It's about negotiation. It's not about resolving conflict, but having social negotiations – like running into a neighbour you wouldn't usually speak to or see. It's forced sociability, as opposed to letting regulations default to the antisocial.

Alban: Minsuk, could you talk about your experience of the protest movements in Seoul? The candlelight demonstrations, for example.

Minsuk: From my experiences with those movements, I have come up with the term *collective intimacy*. *Collective intimacy* depends on cultural differences. In a public space, you're generally more reserved and confined.

In some mass events, we see something different. During the 2002 World Cup, these crazy 'Red Devils' emerged on the street. Seven million fans were in the streets wearing red. People brought their kids, a mix of young men and women, a sweet, massive euphoria.

Graham: I had that exact experience in Vietnam in 2018 when the entire country went out into the city in euphoria after a football win.

Minsuk: A foreign friend who was visiting at the time was shocked. How is this possible? I think this was the very first time that Koreans came out in this fashion. There's a history of violent demonstrations and massacres, as recently as the 1980s, so this was incredibly positive. For the first time, we learnt that large gatherings can be intimate, collective, and peaceful. This was when I decided to return to Korea in 2003.

Slowly, these Korean-style happy hooligans worked their way into political demonstrations. Vicious, fighter activists evolved into something new, and demonstrations turned into family carnival-type events as a form of political protest. The effect was profound. The impeachment protest in 2016 started with about 20,000 mostly professional demonstrators. Slowly, as it got bigger and engaged more people, children, toddlers, baby strollers, it became more like a real carnival with hundreds of thousands and even millions of people. The intimacy found at these events and the social *tightness* is, in part, what caused them to be so successful.

Graham: I want to bring the discussion back to the ideas we touched on earlier. Emma, can you talk about how density features in your research?

Emma: I've been looking at the conditions of remote mining towns in Western Australia, which are often built from scratch to accommodate a large number of people. They take a suburban model as the acceptable unit of living or habitation and build that in the middle of nowhere. This approach is regardless of whether that is an appropriate amount of space per person.

I've been asking: could you build *tighter* even though you have more space? Just because you have space, should you use it? I look at other cities and think of how clumsily we've dealt with the car. We say that the city is about the car, but it's a very clumsy relationship. Walkability and reducing dependence on the car is also a clumsy relationship and hasn't yet led to any more interesting urban outcomes. In high density, you have economic and spatial pressures. But in situations where you don't have those pressures, it's not necessarily the best idea to build big.

Graham: It's a great counterpoint to Japan or Korea because there is always a debate about how much *tightness* is circumstantial. Tsukamoto will talk about the density in Tokyo as being out of necessity. Australians will constantly say they don't need compact cities because of the vast amounts of land. The remote mining towns that Emma is talking about are extreme examples of that approach. It becomes a question – is *tightness* desirable? Even when you're not forced into it economically or spatially.

Donald: The city as a demarcated zone, both as a conceptual and a socio-political entity, says, 'if you go outside this gate, you're no longer a citizen.' But a lot of that was also due to defence. The closer the body is, the smaller the wall has to be in circumference to provide protection. Once ballistics and gunpowder came in, city walls broke down. The suburb conceptually comes after the city wall is no longer necessary. Being outside the wall and still being a citizen – a suburb as opposed to the *urb* – becomes a very charged difference. There are still cultures where compactness is valued for sharing resources – farmlands and water, for instance, also sharing the care of the children and the animals. You still have compactness in village structures that are based on different economics.

David: In the nuclear age, suburbia was actually held up as a model of urbanisation. And in the case that it was bombed, you might still keep three-quarters of the population.

Graham: The new logic of defending yourself by being far apart.

John: Conversations on tight cities so frequently move to war – Tsukamoto often refers to the condition in Tokyo following the second world war.

Minsuk: The publications *Made in Tokyo* and *Post-Bubble City* catalogue the condition of the city in the years following the economic crisis. There were unintended preserved patches in the middle of high-rise buildings. In Shinjuku, there is a wall of tall buildings that forms a ring around neighbourhoods of preserved older buildings. We have to work with governance, politicians, processes of rent stabilisation, and many other aspects beyond architectural solutions to maintain these urban qualities. We also have to be careful. Look at the example of Bukchon, a neighbourhood in Seoul famous for the old traditional Korean houses that have been completely Disney-fied. When you visit, you can even rent traditional costumes to go with the experience. It's insane. Instead of fetishising the existing, there is an opportunity to learn its logic and apply it to new building designs. Christopher Alexander was doing this in the early 1960s.

Graham: Saigon is an example where the economy is charging ahead, and density is going down dramatically. The small houses are being replaced by big footprint offices, and the population is moving outward.

Donald: In China, every project we've ever done had setbacks from five or ten to fifteen metres. It produces a kind of urban density that is not dense. For instance, there is no adjacency – everything has a border. There is a physical quality to *tightness*, which produces offsets and interstitial gaps. This condition is very different to when everything is framed by a bordering system.

John: The kind of urbanism in China that you just described is a model now being exported. But maybe that is the lesson from the examples of your office, Minsuk. We don't just have to rely on the existing urban fabric. We can do new *tight* buildings, and we can do a new type of density really well.

06

Freeze!

Minsuk Cho (Mass Studies)

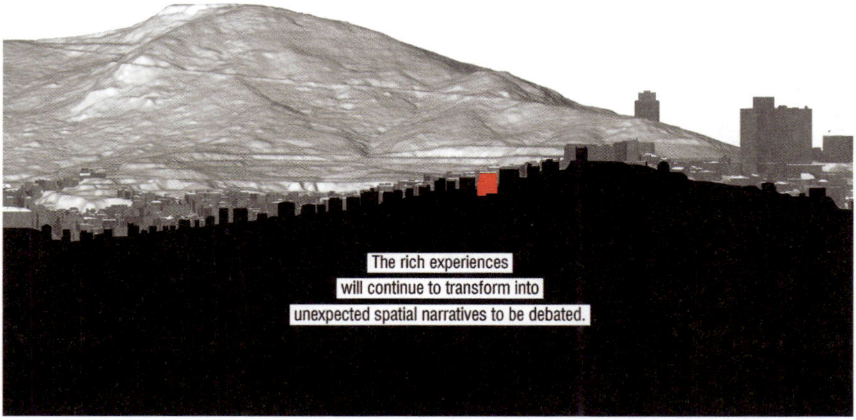

Freeze! explores the relationship of Mass Studies' self-built office space within the district of Itaewon in Seoul. The design performs a series of complex spatial negotiations along its boundaries, navigating the requirements of the planning code, and the desires of its neighbours.

This is a unique experience
for buildings surrounded by
deep, narrow, sectional outdoor spaces,

and still achieve
a better spatial environment
was the main task.

1.06m

A new 4m tall grating fence is built,
opening the new basement level,
letting in natural light.

multiple ground levels
unfound in a tower typology.

1.3m

B1 Mezzanine

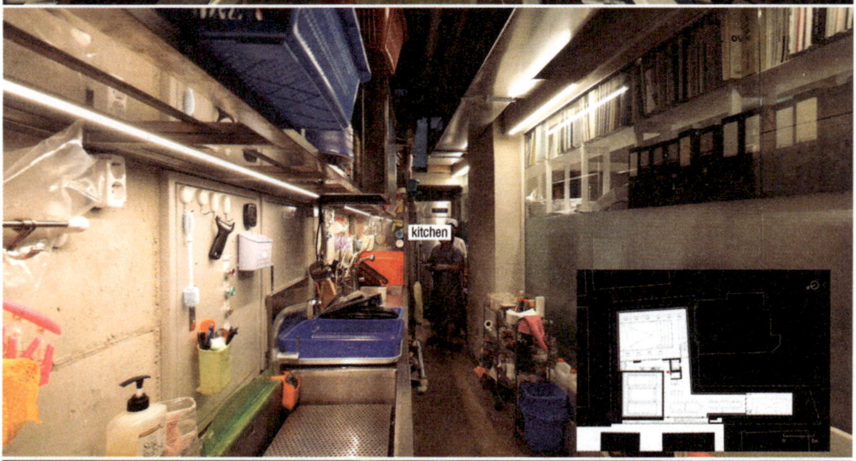
kitchen

farm-to-table

The building is set on a sloping flag shaped site, with neighbouring buildings situated closely on all sides. Many trades and affordances have been made with adjacent structures to allow for the building to expand out and be more *tightly* situated against its neighbours.

A large step down is created to allow light into the basement of the building. The building uses glass on many of the facades opening out on to the interestitial spaces around it, allowing light into the envelope, while at the same time 'borrowing' the walls of neighbouring structures as a kind of urban wallpaper - delighting in the materiality of its surroundings. The project suggests a model of architectural design that contributes an incremental adjustment to the city through a series of small scale and bottom up processes.

07

Rasquachismo & Adjustment or Control & Planning

Analysis of urban *tightness* and density frequently revolves around questions of planning and regulation. Regulated planning can be the mechanism to create density and the mechanism which prevents it. Free market development might claim both, holding the potential to unleash hyper density or facilitate sprawl. By contrast, a process of incremental adjustment or urban *rasquachismo* – a method of making do and recycling might create a *tightness* not possible through the efforts of either the planner or the developer.[1]

The image of a Saigonese couple on a motor scooter negotiating the swarm of Vietnam's traffic is one of the great lessons in urban *tightness*. The experience of that same traffic to the newly arrived tourist usually invokes bewilderment and sometimes terror. Yet being inside that swarm, and especially being inside that swarm on two wheels, is astonishingly manageable; it is a flow that works beyond all the logic of the traffic engineer or urban designer. It is the result of a thousand tiny adjustments, behaviours that grease this subtle and complex machine. Sometimes it is about patience and going slow. Mostly the swarm follows the logic of not stopping, of going around, of swerving or mounting a kerb. Sometimes it means deliberately running against the correct traffic flow – a shortcut made to counter the inconvenient design of the roads. At such close quarters, the vehicles can adjust intuitively; by making eye contact, by getting spatial clues from the next bike, a kind of deafening peloton pursuing different courses but negotiating the same space.

The many adaptations this vehicle swarm makes to the city are a visible expression of a workaround. Packing a motorbike with whatever is needed is a local art form and a celebrated amusement for those same tourists: the driver carrying three tightly-packed children, sometimes with one in front perched on a crate or a stool. Sometimes it is a dog, cargo, eggs, a fridge, potted trees, windows for a high rise facade all stacked with surreal enormity. When there are only two or three people, they often hold close and chat. The term *xe om* used for the traditional bike taxis means bike hug. There are conversations between bikes. Drivers in the swarm are as close to each other as passengers in the carriage of a metro. Food carts set up on the street, and street market stalls alike, cater to bikes who pull up and buy goods while barely stopping. The heavy seasonal rain pauses but does not stop this swarm as purpose-made capes drape over the driver and bike. It is difficult to imagine how this city would operate without this mode of moving; so compact in plan, but also so agile and fluid. A whole network of very narrow streets exist in the ambiguous zone of being trafficable, but not to the car.

Graham Crist
Untitled
Ho Chi Minh City

Archie Pizzini
Rasquachismo Series
Ho Chi Minh City

In 2014, the City of Melbourne published a report on the potential effect of replacing a percentage of cars with motorbikes in the city. The effect, as modelled, was not surprisingly significant and positive for the efficiency of car traffic. The simple numbers of two wheels versus four would free up valuable asphalt. The motorcycle though, creates a grey area between the cyclist, pedestrian and the car.[2] It disrupts the model of the walkable city, creating at times, chaos for the car and also for the pedestrian. Conventional car versus pedestrian equations are seriously challenged in Ho Chi Minh City, where the motorbike is an adjustment down from the car, and a supercharged walker. The recent arrival of large numbers of American SUVs in Vietnamese cities is alarming for this relationship and for the tight swarm. Static traffic and giant cars jamming the narrow lanes become a problem which can only be confronted by urban planning and by demolition. By contrast, the urban scooter is invisible to the master plan. It expresses its capacity for *tightness* through a fluid adjustment to the city, to the swarm of other bikes and in the city's adjustment to it. Often viewed or described as an image of chaos, it is indicative of the capacity of a city to mould, adjust and inflect at its edges.

Rasquachismo is a mode of adaptation and adjustment. The architect and photographer Archie Pizzini has transposed this word to Vietnam and scaled its use to the urban environment of Ho Chi Minh City. There he has repurposed *rasquachismo* to reflect his observations of urban life around him. The term *Rasquache*, coming from the Aztec Nahuatl language, was usually pejorative, inferring both impoverishment and kitsch. It is the term *Rasquachismo* applied to art that has asserted and resurrected its value, identified its aesthetic and described its ethic. It is an aesthetic of exuberant bricolage, an ethic proud of frugality and a culture usually associated with Latin America. For Pizzini, a Texan artist, architect and photographer of Mexican heritage, and now practising in Vietnam, the term and the sensibility resonated vividly in this South-East Asian urban environment. Through the observations of urban life in architectural photography, and his collection of everyday objects made on the streets in Ho Chi Minh City, Pizzini found an intense degree of adaptive ingenuity. *Rasquachismo* is a quick and dirty aesthetic, made from whatever is at hand. Opposed or antithetical to western high minimalism, it expresses the most with the least. The least can at times be almost nothing, an object fashioned from an adjustment to the found.

'Making the most with the least is a statement of irreverence and is both defiant and inventive. '[3]

More broadly than its use in art practice, *rasquache* can refer to the repurposing and valuing of the disposable; of refashioning junk.

Archie Pizzini
Rasquachismo Series
Ho Chi Minh City

Sue Hajdu
Urban Documentation
Vietnam Series
Ho Chi Minh City

Pizzini observes this sensibility in abundance in Ho Chi Minh City and sees its logic scaled from the little objects crafted from refuse, to the organisation of the city. The tendency to recycle and to avoid waste is essential to sustaining contemporary life and it is applicable to urban space where resources are limited.

The vernacular Vietnamese *tube* house is very efficient, both because it has a small land footprint and because the large household makes the space work over several levels. A house on four or five levels with a roof garden above and a series of spaces shared between plenty of children or several family generations with perhaps a business on the ground level is an urban model which relies on negotiation and adjustment. Its planning is at best skeletal, and its use is vaguely defined and redefined. At its most vague is the interface with its urban edges.

The urban fabric of much of Ho Chi Minh City is tightly woven, a fine grain pattern of sites and narrow lanes sitting within a larger layout of boulevards. And yet, through this weave is a third layer: the adjustments to the street pattern by temporary occupation. The micro-enterprises that are set up in the laneways range from the constantly mobile to moveable only when needed. The ambiguity of public space and private use adjusts from morning to evening, from the edge of the street to its centre. All cities do this or attempt to, as a common characteristic of *tight* urban conditions. But here, it is vital and intense in many parts of the city, supported by a combination of a fine physical network of paths and a highly developed culture of semi-regulated micro-vendors. The ingenious and hyper-efficient use of urban space by these many vendors is what Pizzini translates as *Rasquachismo*. It forms a template of use for the network of lane spaces and street edges that swarm and adjust. Paradoxically, this loosely regulated environment can trigger urban *tightness* and is a key ingredient to the small footprint city.

Comparable debates on the re-adjustment of city-scale occur in many places and have been played out intensely in Japan at the turn of the millennium. The *Void Metabolism* described in Yoshiharu Tsukamoto's 2012 essay of the same name inverts the logic of the avant-garde Japanese Metabolism and distributes the dynamism of the metropolis into countless infills and refills.[4] In the Metabolist vision of the 1960s, the service core anchors dynamic and metabolising capsules of space. This image is countered in Tsukamoto's construction by a city growing in on itself through the re-activation of void spaces. It is more than a switch from elevated core to empty plot. The *void metabolism* replaces an image of erasure and reconstruction with one of adjustment and incremental *tightening*.

'...Tokyo is continuously undergoing a process of metabolism – one without cores or capsules, but with voids and small buildings. This 'Void Metabolism' is in contrast to the 'Core Metabolism' of the 1960s. Directly emerging from the conditions of the city, the first generation of Void Metabolism started in the 1920s with the first wave of suburban developments.'[5]

The major works of the Japanese Metabolists in the 1960s described a city set in motion by conceptually abandoning the old city and by figuring a new layer on its ruins. Isozaki's famous *Re-ruined Hiroshima* (1968) dives deep into the territory of the perpetual destruction and re-imagining of the city. Just as Kenzo Tange's master plan for Skopje responded to the devastating 1963 earthquake in Macedonia, Isozaki's *City of the Air* (1962) imagines Shinjuku as similarly ruined with a new modern city hovering over it. His statement on the project is explicit in this:

'Tokyo is hopeless…I am leaving everything below 30 meters to others. If they think they can unravel the mess in this city, let them try. I will think about architecture and the city above 30 meters. An empty lot of 10 square meters is all I need on the ground. I will erect a column there, and that column will be both a structural column and a channel for vertical circulation.'[6]

Unravelling the mess in the city through the adjustment at a tiny scale is precisely the work of the void metabolist. The empty ten square metres of lot which for Isozaki forms an elevating column and core becomes in void metabolism instead, the tiny footprint house. The inner suburbs of Tokyo take this concept to the extreme in the slithers of by-product land that exist between buildings and between buildings and the street. These interstitial spaces, formed by the incremental subdivision of the city from ancient agricultural land to the world's largest metropolis, becomes the site of a highly choreographed, manicured and polite form of Japanese *rasquachismo*. Plants and potted gardens, carefully placed signage, vending machines, tiny shops and other 'pet architectures' occupy the gaps formed from the different setback and regulatory requirements, infrastructural corridors and other urban phenomena. In contrast to the master planned future of the Metabolists, the urban landscape that this infill creates forms the other Tokyo that has since become so well known, which is suburban in origin and which has incrementally *tightened* its voids. The massive destruction of Tokyo was a trigger for re-imagining the city, and the equivalent is true of Paris for Le Corbusier, but in reverse, (where the re-imagining is a trigger for its destruction). That rethinking comes with a master plan and with a seizing control of the city's future.

By contrast, preserving old urban structures, maintaining land ownership patterns and carving off small slices of the city for future generations might seem hopelessly ineffective or conservative.

Yet the *rasquachismo* urbanist approaches, simply shrugs and gets on with what they can - filling voids and making do. It is significant that Isozaki offers to leave everything below thirty metres to others to try and unravel the mess. His position is clear: unravelling the mess is not the work of a master planner nor is it the business of the urban visionary. Perhaps it is simply the work of everyone else to exercise their *rasquachismo*, as it is for those living below the speculative *City of the Air.*

Super Tight reimagines the city at a smaller scale and with less force. *Rasquachismo* reaches only as far as it needs, or as far as it can with its limited means. The destruction or replacement of cities can no longer be a precondition for their re-imagining. The mindset of *rasquachismo* is an antidote to that impulse. Not only is master planning intertwined with urban destruction and replacement, but it appears incapable of real *tightness*. Concerned with unravelling the mess through thinning out or restarting, it is the unplanned adjustments of the master plan which *tighten* and make it dense. To *tighten* a city, we must retain aspects of it which already exist. These are usually at the edges or voids – a metabolism of whatever is leftover within the fabric. *Tightness* is a gradual reconciliation with density through the adjustment of inhabitation.

The adjustment, metabolising or *tightening* impulse of cities is not conservation. The preservation of an historical city or the urban planning controls which seek to replicate that old city are simply a master plan for an imagined past. Just like the master plan for an ideal future, it precludes the adjustment and unplanned *tightening* that we find in the metabolised void, or in the city of *rasquachismo*.

Those on the ground left to unravel the mess are well suited to the task. They have time, and they have scale. Adjusting at one to one beats the distant, coarse lines of the master plan for density and finesse. The voids are metabolised at a finer resolution. Those others on the ground, the micro vendors, their customers on motorbikes, the family on a small plot of land have time on their side. Inhabiting the everyday, inheriting from the last generation, they slowly refine their understanding of the urban space and its *tight* voids. What can the design of *supertight* cities achieve through planning, or rather what can master planning best contribute? It can make space for *rasquachismo*; for the metabolising of voids. It can prevent the developer from monopolising and prevent its own tendency to control and regulate. At its best, the plan can leave space for those others to unravel the mess, and free to attend to the task of adjusting and *tightening*.

08

An interview with photographer Sue Hajdu in Ho Chi Minh City and Melbourne

Sue: Aside from a year-long artists residency in Japan in 2013, I have lived and practiced as an artist in Vietnam since 1994. This is the longest time I've been away from the place in 25 years. In my photographs, I'm trying to find buildings that are significant either because they illustrate something quite generic in an elegant way or sometimes in an extremely ugly way. The sensuality of the city is what appeals to me; cities have a very different sensual vibe to one another. Hanoi feels different to Saigon. This sensuality arises partly from the weirdness of some buildings, but also from the way they juxtapose in extraordinary ways, and sometimes morph into each other. Beautiful forms of juxtaposition can result; buildings that are literally cut in half then get something else attached to them. Saigon was a stunning city of French villas, but after 1975 the population that came to take over the South built shops and shacks and all sorts of little things in the gardens around them.

John: I want to discuss your editing process. You've been able to select from tens of thousands images, and all of these are tightly composed and framed.

Sue: I trained in a very theoretical photography course in Sydney, largely using film. I learned to create singular impressive images on a tripod with expensive film, waiting for the perfect lighting moment. The obsession with getting things perfect stopped me from photographing for years; had it not, I would have started this project way earlier. Then my first digital camera freed me up to take 300 shots in one go. I later bought a proper SLR digital camera, but I no longer stand on a corner for an hour to get the perfect light. I generally shoot in the early morning when the light envelops buildings. The evening gets dusty and too red. I rarely have people in my shots because their heads become black blobs. I get up early when the light is soft – not many motorbikes, not many people, and I shoot lots.

The images that appeal to me most are the ones that become almost abstractions: walls, gates, rusty metal surfaces. Sometimes you get elusive Vietnamese walls with just one window; those are my favourites – a way of focusing in on the one building.

Graham: Your shots have a very lived-in quality. They are unmistakably about people. This is partly to do with the furniture and objects, also the quality of the buildings.

Sue: I'm not so interested in telling stories about people. I'm interested in the buildings as noteworthy and also un-noteworthy forms. But occasionally at 6:00 am, there will be a guy still sleeping on his motorbike on a corner. That's OK.

John: The people are absent from the frame but there is often evidence of someone being in the scene just before the shot was taken.

Sue: People live in those cities and in those buildings. I've focused less on magnificent buildings because Vietnam didn't have that many of them. I've noticed that the buildings in colonial Myanmar are grander than those in Vietnam. I think colonial Myanmar had more money. There isn't that much grandeur in Vietnam. I'm more interested in vernacular, humble buildings. The hodgepodge of lived-in Vietnamese buildings – their human residue, scratches on the wall, decoration or objects.

John: You described the juxtaposition in cities where everything joins up. That seems evident in your photos.

Sue: I don't usually enter these buildings. I'm usually on the outside imagining: Why did that happen? Was it illegal? Sometimes there is a tiny gap which is beautiful.

Graham: The gaps between buildings in Tokyo, for instance, have a clear purpose. English property law has party walls, a way of building to property boundaries that is still very orderly. In Vietnam, there seems to be a much *looser* edge to their property boundary.

Sue: In the early 1990s, Vietnam was a pretty lawless place. There weren't many laws in existence. There was corruption. You could do more or less what you wanted.

John: The buildings in your images are in some way the physical legacy of this period. They are artefacts of culture, of corruption. We don't need the people or the paperwork to prove it. Even in fluid cities that go up and come down relatively quickly, they still have a time span that moves past daily life, a fossilized smoking gun.

Sue: This was amplified in Vietnam: it was a time capsule as a consequence of the American trade embargo. There wasn't much stuff available in Saigon when I first visited, but you could still read the layers of history on the buildings and the city – the wrecked neon signs of American wartime bars or the mid-century French villas. Often the more derelict buildings were more atmospheric. It had shock value to someone from the outside. I suppose you could say the decay had a sensuality.

Graham: In the last five years, there has been an immense amount of generic construction in parts of Saigon. Do you think this nostalgia for decay is a response to these changes?

Sue: There are young people who are starting up businesses of various kinds with an aesthetic that is bringing a different kind of sensuality to the city. They're tapping into world culture and also mining their own past. Since around 2010, there has been a deliberate reappraisal of Saigon's pre-war urban culture.

Graham: Is this a form of rebellion? To be somehow retro? Like the couple I met in their early 20s dressed in flawless 1950s outfits with a gorgeous vintage camera and a beautifully restored 1960s Vespa.

Sue: I don't know if it's rebellious – I know it's political. People after 1975 grew up with books and records from the previous era having been taken out of circulation.

At one point, Tan Son Nhat was the busiest airport in the world, with goods coming into the country from everywhere. Everything was available because of an artificial American presence. Urban popular culture and a very strong intellectual culture existed. Some older Saigonese see French Saigon of the 1950s and 1960s as a golden age. Twenty years ago, it would have been seen as suspect behaviour to mine these parts of history.

Graham: There now seems to be a densely built city versus a starkly different but densely inhabited city. Have you made any observations of the bundles of new towers in District 2?

Sue: No, I haven't done much. I'm not sure why these developments are being built, but the investment is coming from places like Singapore and Korea.

John: It's a global phenomenon. We often see towers being built but not inhabited in any way similar to *hẻms*, for instance.

Sue: Yes, if you consider floor space, they're not particularly dense, compared to what people have been living in previously.

Graham: This is part of the challenge for a culture transitioning to car parks, supermarkets, apartment towers, and a subway system.

Sue: When I first arrived, there was no bus system. They had just dismantled the old French trams in Hanoi. Now, they're building a metro that physically disciplines the population. Riding a motorbike is like riding your horse in the Wild West. You go where you want – up on the pavement, in and out of buildings, sometimes against traffic. There is a schedule for the bus, and there are points to conform to – like the factory schedule. The metro is formalising these things. We're seeing the gradual disciplining of the Vietnamese population.

John: That has been described in European culture as well.

Sue: In the past, it was common for men to take time off work whenever they wanted. They might turn up at the shop or office and then go off for a few hours to cafes; even a police officer would do that. That was the norm. You could do whatever you wanted. You could have a desk job and a related business which you could run through there. A $40-a-month desk job was just a convenient way to do all the other things that you do during your eight-hour day.

Graham: A colleague has described how the majority of Hanoi's street-front businesses are the family's second business to supplement the salary income.

Sue: Yes, but in these new apartment blocks, you see formalising rules – tracking identities, cards, taking your photo when you arrive on your motorbike. You now turn up on time for work, and you stay there. The pattern I just described is less frequent now.

Graham: The *hẻms* still get busy just after 9:00 am though – people turn up for work, settle in and then go and have a coffee or breakfast. Perhaps it's a less regulated urban environment in laneways. I am curious about the gated laneways that you see in other cities like Ahmedabad.

Sue: Here, it is literally a boom gate.

Graham: Sometimes a boom gate and sometimes the actual swinging gate with a sign across the top. Although, I have never seen these gates closed.

Sue: They usually close for the curfew. It can also happen with older 1950s apartment blocks that are organised in a courtyard. The curfew is fairly early, about 11:00 pm. There is a guy who lives in a little room at the front that manages it. If you are locked out, you may not have the key yourself. In some cases, if you know you are going out partying, you might make a special deal – you tell him: 'I'm going to be back late.' It works in different ways. I have friends that know they're going to be locked out, so they just stay out all night.

Graham: I knew an apartment where the gate to the laneway was a front door and was padlocked. You could neither get in nor out.

Sue: Sometimes there are security concerns in alleyways. For eight years, I lived in an area that was known for drug addicts, dealers, and criminals. I was taught to be careful. There are also "polite" alleyways where nothing happens. They are spic and span like a suburban street. There might be pot plants but no street life. In my *hẻm*, people's daily lives spilled out and beyond the doorstep. The houses were tiny; just to get air and sunshine and see people, you'd be outside your front door. Women would go every morning and buy their vegetables and come home. Without much TV or radio, bars or travel, what are you going to do for entertainment? Sit on that doorstep, and have a good gossip all day.

Strictly speaking, your ownership is the floor area of your house. If you've been living there for decades, a lot of your daily life extends into the street. In contrast to those "polite" alleyways, these spaces are often where people might have a food stall in the afternoon or a lunchtime store. A hell of a lot of food preparation happens out there for commercial purposes, not for domestic purposes. By inhabiting that space for a large portion of most days, except Sundays, it becomes *my space* – even though it's technically public space.

Graham: It is ownership through presence, the opposite of apartment buildings, where owners who don't live in the country have a controlling say over it.

Sue: And this presence and habit is not chaos, it has its own internal logic. Most people don't follow the rules so much, it's the customs that matter. Western societies are hyper regulated compared to Vietnam. Building regulations or traffic laws count less than customary inhabitation. If you said, 'Hey, but according to the law...!' in Vietnam, you would be seen as just being argumentative or talking nonsense.

Graham: And arguably you would be.

THANH HÓA

09

Urban Documentation Vietnam Series (2009-2019)

Sue Hajdu

Over a number of years photographer Sue Hajdu has carefully documented the changes in Vietnam's cities, and the subtle adjustments to space in everyday life. Often captured in early morning soft light, the empty spaces mark their tight inhabitation through the arrangement of objects. The precise composition of the series reflects Hajdu's formal training in Australia, and her detailed knowledge of Vietnam developed since her arrival there in the 1990s.

101
FO
KEM
FO
TO
BÁN
THẺ
FOTO
KEM - SỮA CHUA
VINAMILK

UYÊN COFFEE
The No.1 Coffee
TRÚC MAI
TÂN ĐẠT

TONY
Kodak
TIỆM VÀNG
KIM HÒA Minh

13

SƠN

10

An interview with architect and photographer Archie Pizzini, Vietnam

Archie: In Texas, I was given an antique, medium format camera. I then started documenting abandoned factories and repair yards. When I came to Vietnam, I lost access to my darkroom, so I went digital. Vietnam was so stimulating I impulsively took photographs. I didn't know what I was documenting, but it was all incredibly fascinating. I took thousands of photos and was thinking about making a book, without knowing what to call it. It was years before I could make sense of everything I had seen and a long time before I collected the thousands of photos and was thinking about a book. My PhD pulled all of these photographs together into a larger picture of the city and how it relates to globalised society.

Graham: Your angle on the *super tight* is informed by Vietnam's cities and how they contrast with American cities that you know.

Archie: My focus on *tight* space relates to *rasquachismo* – the term for making what everyone needs out of whatever is at hand. It is tied to reuse, repair, and improvisation. You see this very much in Vietnam, as well as India and Mexico. Any place where people with limited resources make stuff. *Rasquachismo* infuses *tight* neighbourhoods. It is trying to make do with tiny living or retail spaces, continuously modifying a found object to fit. The result is sustainable and socially beneficial. The upsides deserve to be studied. I have photographed particular districts of Ho Chi Minh City with very dense alleys where you might find a market for used motorbike parts or working shophouses. I focused on strategies of improvisation that make these living arrangements work. The ingenuity produces things where you can see all the forces at work.

Graham: I'm wondering what your sense of the improvised means for planning environments in the way that architects would understand.

Archie: Improvisation comes into the way of living with *tightness* in the social and urban fabric. For example, it is handling social interactions that are close to you but don't include you.

It requires an invisible wall to say, 'I'm not part of this' but allow it to happen. Conversely weddings, parties and funerals occur in the *hẻms*, and they include neighbours because they have to. Improvisations architecturally and socially are inseparable. In globalised societies, we tend to get separated from each other. Elderly care and child care is dependent on an outside entity. But *Tight* neighbourhoods tend to be interdependent with a safety net of human connections.

Graham: *Rasquachismo* is often described pejoratively in its association with poverty. How do you detach its negative connotations?

Archie: I've seen people who are proud of it, some who are ashamed of it. My grandfather from Mexico arrived in America, taught himself to repair shoes, bought a house, and then added a shoe shop and rent houses. He built them with his own hands, taught himself everything, just kept building and improvising. *Rasquachismo* is a substitution of ingenuity for money. Repairing things is important for sustainability. Large corporations have been called out on actively impairing the ability to repair and modify their devices. It is deliberately wasteful.

John: You're describing a type of empowerment through access to the built environment and physical objects.

Archie: Empowerment happens at a basic level through direct communication. It is turning your head to the person next to you and opening your mouth. Proximity leads to empowerment, ideas, bonding, and connection between generations. The median age in Vietnam was just twenty-five when I got here in 2005. It is still very young, and it is changing fast.

John: In Japan, it's around sixty-eight.

Graham: There is a very rapid adoption of new ideas in Vietnam – technologies, iPhones, big cars.

Archie: Development is also subtracting the physical spaces interdependent with the economics of very small businesses. World bank figures from 2010 say that sixty-five per cent of employed Vietnamese were self-employed. The United States listed less than ten per cent. There is a market for small lease spaces in a dense area, meaning the economics lines up with density. In these areas, everything is within walking distance. You have few cars going through there. Different types of vehicles exist for these tight spaces - the cyclo, the motorbike, the tricycles, pushcarts – all designed to navigate small alleyways. These neighbourhoods are being replaced with towers, but a dense neighbourhood doesn't work in a tower.

Graham: There are two distinct layers: the city of *hẻms* and the towers that continue to appear at an astonishing rate. Do you observe the capacity for this culture to adjust to the recently built towers? Are there high-rise versions of the *hẻm tightness*? Is it a characteristic of those towers that they are built not to be adjusted?

Archie: The new ones I've seen are not being adjusted. There are some cases of the older towers from the 1960s being used in a *hẻm*-like way. Some have four-metre wide corridors, plenty of ventilation and natural light.

Graham: It is a paradox to suggest that adjustments can work if the corridor is wider than normal and wider than many of the low rise *hẻms*.

Archie: To achieve real density, you also need smaller apartments. At the moment, the finances are geared towards larger apartments.

Graham: It is interesting that there is development pressure at all since some of Saigon's districts are the densest in the world. Often arguments for regeneration are based around beautification or health benefits. You're describing development that is decreasing density.

Archie: The density is decreasing, yet there is a view that Saigon needs to accommodate more people. The projected growth of Saigon over the next ten years is another 10 million. *We need to grow upward* was the discussion five years ago. This approach is de-densifying the incredibly dense neighbourhoods which undercuts the stated aim.

Graham: Though the stated aim is also to create open space and the amenity that western planners value. Open, but not necessarily public.

John: Do you consider *hẻms* to be public space?

Archie: Yes. There is an idea that *hẻms* are an abnormal phenomenon, but really they are one of the last examples of the normal usage of a street before motor vehicles. It is a public space, and people use it as a private space. It is a swing space, and the edges become fuzzy. People open the front ends of their houses and also occupy the opposite side of the *hẻm*. This blurriness is public in the sense that it is sort of everybody's, and if you need it, you use it.

Graham: The terms *fuzzy* or *blurry* seem important to the ownership.

John: As long as you're there, it's yours. As soon as you leave, your presence is broken, and it passes on to someone else. Quite different to cities like New York, for example, where a staggering percentage of the city is vacant as it is owned by oligarchs or absent investors.

Graham: In your own *hẻm* in Saigon Archie, the presence and ownership is partly the result of relocation from the North in 1975 after the war. People resumed property titles and acquired vacated houses. Many of these spaces seem very fluid.

Archie: Property ownership here is complicated. Ownership never goes to the individual: the land belongs to the people, and what you buy is the right to use it. For foreigners, you buy that right for a set number of years. But when the first Europeans came to America, the Native people thought this European idea of ownership was crazy. How could you possibly own the land?

It has existed forever and you're going to be gone in a few decades. It was such an odd idea. That sort of view has some utility in the way we treat our cities and our planet.

Graham: So what are the ingredients for a 21st century tight city?

Archie: The word *necessary* is where it all hinges. The idea of a need has been subverted. There is a *need* for something if you can get somebody to buy it, but a need is really something of basic benefit to people that they cannot do without. The *tight* city I would like to make would be more interconnected between people – this quality is missing more and more. The clues from the *super tight* neighbourhoods of Vietnam are the way they promote these social connections. They are not paradise, but there are qualities about these neighbourhoods that could be adapted to benefit new cities. Things some urban designers are advocating for in American cities already exist in Vietnam but are being lost. It must be understood that street occupation and sociability is intertwined with the economics of how people are employed.

Graham: Some western cities are agonising over creating things that are being removed in Saigon as we speak.

Archie: Yes, and I experienced it from the other direction, through my elderly parents in Texas. They were fine, but slowing down. And they didn't cook anymore and drove out every day for food in their car. They reached a point where they could no longer drive. Nobody delivered food in their large suburb, and the nearest place to buy food was further than they could walk. And they knew none of their neighbors well. It was a real life-threatening crisis.

In my own *hẻm*, there are four or five places within sight of our door where you can eat. You could pick up the phone, and people would deliver it. It's very instructive to consider which is a more advanced type of city.

John: We're effectively trying to put a number or a value on proximity. In your case density becomes a lifesaver.

Graham: I am still curious about the necessary ingredients or the spice. While there is acknowledgement amongst urbanists about walkable cities and fine grain density, these don't generally produce a Vietnamese *hẻm*. It has qualities that don't fit a standard formula of walkable urbanism. It's a little wilder.

Archie: There is a lot of open-air stuff, and traditionally a tolerance for unconditioned spaces. There is also a common experience of American visitors being over-stimulated by this city; it is simply too much to experience, but it stimulates the capacity to imagine such places. It took me a long time to understand what was happening in the Vietnamese *hẻms*, how economics and social behaviours all came together to participate in this *tightness*. A lot of new developments in the world are being designed by people who perhaps have never seen or experienced a real city of this type. What they have experienced doesn't allow them to imagine this reality.

11

Rasquachismo Series

Archie Pizzini

A series of hems or alleys off of Yersin Street are home to an aromatic group of spice stalls lining passageways so tiny that they resemble tunnels more than alleys. Other local shops sell kitchen needs, other edibles, hats and fans, and altar supplies.

Pizzini's images capture the resourcefulness and the intimacy of living closely, often in material poverty and social richness. In every case, the human figure, inhabitant of their urban space, is the central point of the picture. As an architect, artist and photographer living in Saigon, he has been closely observing that city's qualities with deepening affection – qualities which he sees as the antithesis of his native Houston, and more akin to the Mexican culture of his heritage.

This small neighborhood, and its sister neighborhood between Co Bac and Co Giang streets, doesn't rise more than four levels above the street, yet its alleys stay cool on hot days and the deafening din of the adjoining highways and boulevards can't penetrate the quiet of its *hẻms*.

The neighborhood is a showcase of numerous individually improvised architectural solutions and these bestow an organic feel to the city fabric. The neighborhood literally seems to grow, evolve and interconnect itself.

177

The dense neighborhoods of Vietnam, and the tiny spaces it is made up of, necessitate a blurring of public alley space and private indoor space that is compounded by the moving of daily work and family events to the adjoining streets.

Even in District 1, the old colonial city of Sai Gon that is now an epicenter of globalization in Ho Chi Minh City, some neighborhoods still possess the density to support a deeply local and networked life.

Events such as birthday parties, engagement and wedding parties and even funerals happen in the streets and necessarily involve the community. Funerals run several days with evening events that change nightly, sometimes including singers, performers and even acrobats and fire eaters to entertain the children.

Annual celebrations at the Dinh (community halls) often include traditional *hat boi* (traditional Vietnamese opera) performances.

Cho Lon's density supports hundreds of tiny sidewalk coffee and food shops, some in alleys or *hẻms* and some in doorways.

Districts 5 and 6 of Ho Chi Minh City contain Cho Lon, once a small city independent of Sai Gon. Settled by Chinese who migrated to the area during a period of turmoil in China, Cho Lon gained a reputation as a center of commerce reflected by its name which translates literally as "Big Market". It remains an area where you can find nearly everything, from plastic flowers to tools and hardware to industrial scales to children's toys.

MAI HIEN

CLEAR
Dove
BIS
Tide
ARIEL

For those living in the housing blocks, a daily market offering fresh fish, meat, vegetables and fruits as well as soups, coffee stands, sandwiches and noodle dishes lies just downstairs from their apartments.

Beauty shops, repair shops, jewelry and clothing shops, sewing supplies and kitchenware are all mere steps away.

Density, repair and improvisation are integral parts of the *supertight* neighborhoods of Vietnam and have supported the low carbon footprint of Vietnam of the recent past. As Vietnam's cities modernize, that footprint is rising and, though neighborhoods are changing from a four storey city texture to a landscape of twenty and thirty storey towers, density in population is actually decreasing.

Vietnam's sustainability advantage is decreasing as its cities become more like those in the globalized world. According to World Bank figures, Vietnam's carbon footprint has risen from about 0.4 tonnes per capita in 1995 to about 1.8 tonnes in 2014.

The small sizes of the homes and shops enable the density and economies that allow such a rich variety of offerings. This provides a visible equation in built form showing how city fabric of dense and tiny spaces supports a greater variety of businesses and builds a stronger social network. These *supertight* Vietnamese neighborhoods are far from perfect, but they have demonstrable advantages that it would benefit all designers to understand.

They build strong social networks, the antithesis of many globalized cities today and ensure that people interact across a broad spectrum of the population regardless of economic, religious, sociological and political groupings; counteracting the polarization of society rising in many less dense and more globalized cities.They support their entrepreneurial and largely self-employed population through the provision of small shop spaces and truly public space, providing the day to day street life that many city planners covet but continually fall short of in contemporary city design.

They reinforce a culture of small scale, local supply, and repair orientation; reinforcing a lifestyle inherently thrifty, sustainable, resilient and less wasteful. These are exactly the qualities that many micro-entrepreneurs and their clients are turning to in their efforts to make society that benefits individuals as well as the planet.The older and dense neighborhoods of Ho Chi Minh City work outstandingly in many ways and should be studied at length and understood by design professionals who are able to view them not as "chaos" to be eradicated, but as supremely relevant case studies in how a society with many desirable aspects evolved a city fabric to serve itself. This city fabric is a detailed reflection of the society that produced it.

12

A conversation with Aleesha Callahan, Editor of Habitus, Indesign Media Asia, Ian Nazareth from RMIT University and Nick Bourns from NH Architecture

Graham: Urban density is often framed as something that planning needs to limit or disperse. The origins of urban planning lie in controlling overcrowding. Now, the health effects of dispersed cities have become more extreme than problems of overcrowding. Nineteenth-century cities controlled diseases spread in close compact populations, and now we see the health effects of loneliness and social dislocation. Most of us have experienced the dislocation of the big city. The health impacts of loneliness are now comparable with smoking or obesity. Correlations between loneliness and urban density are not clear, but let's think of *tightness* as a social form; social cohesion plus density.

Aleesha: It is not just older demographics who suffer from loneliness: research has shown how young people are also struggling with loneliness. There are probably multiple reasons for this development, and I don't necessarily know what role urban design has in its formation. The digital interfaces that we're confronted with are contributing as much as urban form.

Ian: Loneliness maps into bigger public health issues, and it has now been identified as a key risk for the healthcare system. Design is often left on the periphery of these discussions. There has been an obsession with individualised public spaces in public: places where people can go away and use a tablet or a phone in private. We have to think about reversing that paradigm. Over time, the suburban home has pulled every public social function into the house. How do we take it out of the house? This question ties not only into loneliness but other issues, like ageing.

Aleesha: Mixed-use is important to this discussion. Designers and architects like to talk about mixed-use, but I don't know a truly mixed-use space that has been done well. Is it a cultural thing to avoid socialising outside of safe areas, whether home or the office? How do you encourage people to interact in urban areas that are genuinely mixed?

Ian: We can analyse which spaces work and make some conclusions. If we start to throw this lens on the city, we can understand how good spaces encourage particular behaviours. It is then possible to determine the qualities we would like to replicate in these mixed-use settings.

Graham: The *super tight* tendency is to start with basic questions about proximity. The premise that some level of proximity is probably not sufficient but is a necessary condition for social interaction. The simplest problem we have with a lot of cities is there isn't enough proximity. People are physically too separated.

Ian: Part of the problem is this idea of the peripatetic digital nomad. In Europe, it is likely that before you're twenty-five you have already lived in three or four different cities. Moving a lot and more often means that populations are connected to a digital network, not a physical network. We see this with new student accommodation; there is almost no identity in the units themselves, but the focus is on shared spaces built into the fabric.

Aleesha: If developers are building student housing accommodation and it's about packing in as many occupants as possible, are they willing or able to give enough space for the inhabitants to actually create social bonds? I'm sure there are great examples, but in a lot of the recent versions that has been forgotten.

Ian: These sorts of public provisions cannot be left up to private development, they have to be understood as part of broader design agendas.

Aleesha: And minimum housing standards have not necessarily done that at all.

Graham: It is interesting how often such discussions go to minimum standards and government regulatory control. Could it be just as much a problem if we created too much space? Is a house being too large as much of a problem as being too small?

Aleesha: Perhaps. We could also borrow from co-working spaces and have community managers whose full-time job is to try and curate a sense of community within the residence. They manage those social areas, ensure they are looked after, even host events and keep them active.

Graham: Tsukamoto's work in Tokyo suggests that ownership is very strongly related to belonging. In Tokyo, density is largely created through very small footprint houses as opposed to high-rise buildings. The idea that you maintain a sense of ownership through the single dwelling, but it is more compressed spatially, seems to be what that body of work advocates.

Aleesha: Is there a fear of small spaces in the dream of a block and garden? What is a place for flexibility and sharing? Is there a place left empty where people fill in the blanks?

Graham: Mark Jacques gave a provocative comment recently on sharing. He suggested that western culture is generally terrible at sharing and is obsessed with protecting its own turf. The optimism you described in relation to millennials sharing space is counterbalanced by the obsession with private property. We lock people up off-shore to protect our national property. Can designers more actively participate in a culture of sharing? Many things described as *super tight* involve people making their own environment and keeping the architects out. Designers instead are serving an owner who wants the maximum amount of space for their money.

Ian: The real estate model is so archaic. Soon we will see more of the sharing economy and subscription. The next step is to find out how you share things. How can a library change? How does a community hall change? Looking at the city as an advanced scheduling system, can we find efficiencies and redundancies rather than building new things? Imagine a working version of a timetabling system where you can have buildings running space more efficiently. Formal spaces can be used more intensely and better utilised.

Graham: For efficiency, we could simply buy less stuff. When the economy is built on buying more stuff, those efficiencies work against this idea. Archie Pizzini describes dispersed Houston, his home city, as deliberately isolating. It is a series of techniques to make us buy more. It is this crude: the more we share, the less we have to buy, and that's a problem for the city's economy. Andy Fergus has described Melbourne as an extreme example of a two-speed design economy. A combination of low-rise sprawl and a super dense high-rise core – horizontal and vertical sprawl. The missing middle band in this scenario is often discussed.

Aleesha: Density shouldn't infer intensified isolation. You can have interconnected, highly efficient ways of operating a city.

Ian: It comes down to the quality of the density. When Rob Adams talked about increasing Melbourne's density, his exemplar is Barcelona – a low-rise, six-story form that has five times the density of Melbourne. It is not the binary of extremely low density and the super-high density – it requires a diverse solution.

Aleesha: Does Barcelona have lower rates of loneliness and more social interaction than a less dispersed city?

Graham: Mental distress rates in cities are known to be higher in the English speaking world than in continental Europe. There are debates as to why this is occurring. Is that urban dispersal or simply inequality? Both are generally greater in the Anglosphere than in Europe and perhaps beyond what architects can influence. *Tightness* becomes entangled in a very broad range of questions. The *Super Tight* project was conscious not to be romantic about hyperdensity but also counter this romantic image of European density with Asian density. *Tightness* tries to capture a perception of density; moving around the city is an indicator of how dense a city feels as opposed to its actual density. You can be comfortable in a dense city if you're not commuting across it in a car. You can be in a low-density city traffic jam every morning, which makes the city feel overcrowded.

Aleesha: Commuting can be OK if your workday starts when you leave for work. We can create transport that enables working; turn it into a third space. But by 2050, the number of people over 80 will triple. How do they get around a dense city more quickly, without disrupting the flow of the city?

Ian: In about twenty years, the percentage of older people will be more than those in their twenties. This change will also alter what we value in a city. Mobility is obviously one of the primary issues. Of course, initiatives such as autonomous vehicles will at some point alleviate some of that mobility pressure. A lot of architecture and urban design has been modelled on the single-family unit, which is ageing. One person is left in a house that previously had four or five, so loneliness is a big concern as well as an aversion to giving up or sharing wealth. We've got diverse households, but housing is still being designed for the traditional high-income households or families.

Graham: It is not really designed for anyone. There is a very *loose* fit between who we design for and who occupies the housing. Most apartments in our city are two bedrooms ideally designed for two single people. Almost none of them have two single people in them. Sometimes they have six, sometimes two couples, often empty. Is that even a design problem?

Aleesha: And how prescribed do you make the design? Do you give a shell and then let people create what would suit them? In Europe, you can rent a basic box; you can put your kitchen in, everything in, and then you take it when you leave.

Graham: Built environments are inherently less fluid than the social organisations we're describing. Nearly all of the future cities already exist unless we demolish and start again, and we've tried this approach. Fifty years from now, we're going to be refitting a whole lot of building stock. *Tightness* is people inhabiting and adjusting cities incrementally over time. Tsukamoto described this process so well in Tokyo.

Aleesha: Fifty years to become familiar with smaller and smaller amounts of space, so it's not such a shock.

Graham: Two-bedroom apartments are still going to be there, and there is going to be a different social structure living in them. They will have to adapt. Same with those three-bedroom houses in the suburbs. Either demolish them and start again or adapt how we live in them.

Aleesha: Assemble are doing a rent to buy model that is reverse engineered. So they are looking at salary incomes, how people can pay a maximum of 30% of their earnings towards rent, and taking away things to make sure that the house can fit how much they can afford. I'm interested to see how that develops. They say they have 200 apartments and over 3,000 people on the waiting list.

Ian: Perhaps the way to intervene in this condition is to reinvent the model or have multiple models to draw on. It is not only a formal design question; it is designing the back-end of viability. It is designing the principles and the means. If you wanted to purchase a compressed, small apartment, you wouldn't even get a loan for it because it's below the threshold of what banks are financing. You can build all the really *tight* apartments you want, but no one is going to be able to buy them. You have to step outside of your expertise or your role as a designer to ask, how does this fit into the broader system?

Aleesha: These models are great, and every architect knows about them, but how do you get them out to a wider audience? How does the everyday person discover initiatives like *Nightingale*?

Graham: The interest in dwellings is often intense; there might be intense talk about a forty square metre apartment, and nothing said about the street outside it. The dwelling is the piece that designers control; town planning schemes tell us what we can do in it, yet the very large area beyond it has less said about it.

Vietnam has a strong culture of micro-enterprises operating in the streets. They supplement salaries and family incomes. They're an important part of the street content, and they parallel the Melbourne laneway and small bar culture. The impulse to control enterprise and its public space conflicts with this street culture.

Nick: When you're looking at a place, and you're performing a mental or actual health check, what kind of qualities of density are you looking for? Are there types? Do you have a health check that you go through when you look at a place?

Ian: There are a couple. Firstly, we can look at a system to understand how it operates at a street level. The good examples treat architecture as a part of the city and proximity to a transport system is an indication and variable of how you think about development. Secondly, there is diversity in the client or the user group for the buildings and surrounding outdoor spaces. One issue is density, the other is intensity, which is more about different kinds of things happening. Density could mean a lot of one thing.

Graham: I would put it even more crudely – Jeff Speck's walkability index. The easiest health check for any city is how easy it is to walk around. Things flow on from that initial idea: intensely overlapped lifestyles and businesses; different in the morning compared with the evening. That is a kind of health check. Are there people living there? Are there things other than living going on there? Can you walk there? Is it different in the morning and the night?

Aleesha: How do you see mixed-use formats changing? Traditionally, it is retail and residential, but what about work plus hotel, workplace plus retail – there are so many different combinations.

Graham: Some hybrids are so straightforward we barely talk about them. Combining a workplace with a hotel or converting one to the other is easy.

Some of it is to do with planning control. In some places, it is very straightforward to legally have a noodle shop in the front room of your house. In other parts of the world, it is impossible. There was a Nike shop operating in my laneway in Saigon. I didn't believe it was there, but it appeared on Google Maps. It was a neighbour's house and a Nike shop. Co-work spaces barely existed ten years ago; the nature of Wi-Fi makes it easier to work flexibly. Some say the problem is less control or regulation; if you leave it to the market, the city will sprawl. Planning regulations have generally dispersed the city, yet planners will often say without control, and if we leave it to the market, we will also get sprawl.

Aleesha: Yes, lots of cool stuff happens when it is not regulated.

Graham: The dilemma for local governments is making places like the Brunswick Design District. They want cool stuff to happen yet think they need to plan and control it because the market doesn't let it happen.

Nick: Universities manage certain responsibilities like regulations and industry, and at the same time trial and test new ideas. One example of this is the opportunity for universities to create and study residential housing.

Graham: Everyone can try innovation – universities or developers. There is an important task to gather information on all the great stuff that doesn't fit codes or the great housing that wouldn't meet minimums and so on.

Ian: Aside from how regulations work, it is also about risk. It asks, how will risk be absorbed in the model? A city council? Developers? The residents who believe in that model?

Aleesha: Architecture and urban planning are so slow moving, you can't instil change overnight.

Great Taste
at
Lee Theatre
24 hrs
全日
BVLGARI

13

The Appearance of the Tight City

Tightness has a relationship to the form and appearance of buildings, cities and the built environment. Several example projects introduce ways of understanding the spatial consequences of density that look beyond issues of human occupation and attempt to describe the formal properties of tightness. Each will explore how architectural form, material and organisation might be considered tight or trigger perceptions of tightness in the experience of the city. The text also focuses on developing a language for describing the physical and formal properties of dense cities. While *tightness* is often associated with austerity or a lack of generosity, it might equally offer strategies for generating opportunity in constrained conditions. By consequence, acts of adjustment and addition can result in urban generosity.

The Super Tight exhibition investigated the role that design and creative practice play in their formation and operation of cities. When we think about urbanism, there is a tendency to talk in generalities or abstractions as a means of distilling vast and heterogenous situations into comprehensible chunks or shorthand ideas. This is not an unreasonable response as the sheer scale and complexity of cities are often overwhelming – particularly for a public audience.

In order to reflect on the role of designers operating in dense urban environments and speculate on the material and spatial qualities of *super tight* conditions, it was essential to develop a means for testing ideas that did not depart from the real and immediate. We loosely describe this process as *versioning* or *modelling* - a set of procedures that use existing spaces within a city to distil key spatial and organisation qualities. These formal analogues contain the lessons of their city. The ambition of these operations is to set aside any nostalgia or sentimentality for the highly particular or unique circumstances of urban environments along with issues of representation and the copy. Instead, we sought to focus on the formal and organisational properties that can be quantified. These include proportions, scale, composition and articulation and how these properties relate to the human body and furniture. We sought to assess the agency of these prototypes to shape the experience of space and their performative qualities in terms of human occupation.

Scale was critical to this understanding. While countless iterations of the exhibition installations were produced using the standard means of architectural design production (scaled drawings, 3D visualisation, physical models), the completion and occupation of the exhibition itself revealed the importance of the 1:1 in assessing the characteristics of the *super tight* as a formal condition.

Vicki Jones
Super Tight Exhibition
Melbourne

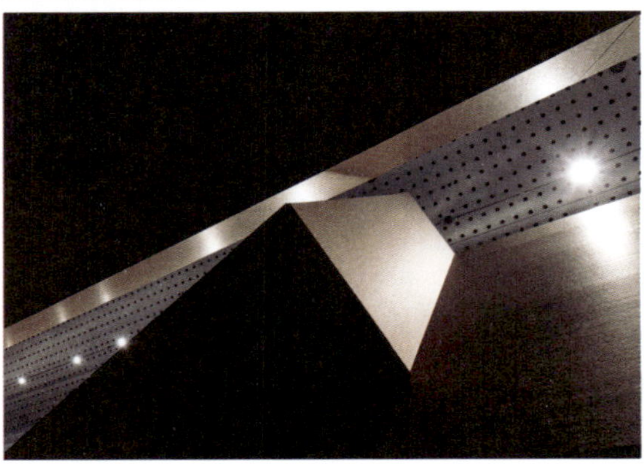

Tobias Titz
Super Tight Exhibition
Melbourne

In particular, it revealed a series of inherent or unconscious biases that we as designers carried with us. What often appeared unreasonably small on paper was surprisingly functional and practical when built. The parts of the installations where space was pinched, compressed or squeezed became the areas where visitors gravitated, forming bottlenecks and moments of negotiation and engagement amongst individuals.

The capacity for these spaces to accommodate people was far greater than we had anticipated during the design phase. In many cases, it was only social customs and behavioural expectations that limited their capacity. The Super Tight project demonstrates that a *tight* form is not simply small but one that precisely aligns its organisation and scale to the performative potential of its use.

The concept of *super tight* has broadened to contain many conditions, perhaps its most clear manifestation is in the small footprint buildings and micro-dwellings in cities such as Tokyo, Hong Kong, Ho Chi Minh City and Seoul. The exhibition takes many of its formal cues from these kinds of spaces, most notably the laneways (*hẻms)* of Ho Chi Minh City and the tiny bars of Tokyo.

The work of co-curator Yoshiharu Tsukamoto's practice Atelier Bow-Wow provides a primer for understanding and identifying the qualities of the *super tight*. Over 30 years, Atelier Bow-Wow has worked within what they describe as the fourth generation of suburban housing in Tokyo. As the city incrementally subdivided from generation to generation, the average plot size has become exponentially smaller. At the same time, the vast sprawl of the city has driven many young professionals to accept and actively seek smaller housing closer to the urban centre. In response to this condition, the practice has produced several houses on tiny footprints, with constrained circumstances that contend with these challenges.

House Tower (2006) was exhibited in the Super Tight exhibition as a large format sectional drawing at 1:2 scale. The project is a four-storey family home on a 42m2 site in the inner city district of Shinagawa, Tokyo. The volume of the house is setback from the front and sides to address planning regulations, leaving a building footprint of 18m2. The most notable aspect of the design, and the reason it was selected for the exhibition, is the way these tight constraints have vertically reoriented the internal planning. As is the case with many of Atelier Bow-Wow's houses, the habitable space is organised sequentially around a staircase on a series of offset split levels that each accommodate a domestic function within a single, continuous vertical volume.

Atelier Bow-wow
House Tower
Tokyo

Sanuki Daisuke Architects
Hẻm House
Ho Chi Minh City

The project contends with the physical and regulatory constraints of the site in a *tight* manner. In plan, it appears tiny, but the section feels vast and voluminous. For example, the study room occupies little more than a borrowed corridor space, but if we reorient the section 90 degrees, the implied footprint is very large. The double-height space contains a bookshelf and opens onto the bedroom platform above, providing a spatial generosity that transcends traditional understandings and measures of comfort in dwellings. The paradox here is that the openness and generosity created within an extremely small space requires a degree of organisational *looseness*. There is very limited functional zoning within the house, other than areas delineated by the stepped platforms. The spaces are loosely distinguished, barely partitioned and configured to allow a variety of household living configurations within *tighter* means. In constrained settings like these, the architect has to fold together temporal layers of behaviour and find a *looseness* within the *tight* crush.

The Hẻm House (2015) by Sanuki Daisuke Architects shares a similar vertical orientation to the House Tower. The dwelling is located at the intersection between two narrow *hẻms*, or laneways, in Ho Chi Minh City. Like the House Tower, the functions are stacked by level, however, the physical constraints allow for a more familiar sequence and set of relationships between functional spaces and circulation. The Hẻm House is embedded within an urban context of vertical tube housing ubiquitous to Ho Chi Minh City. These houses are tightly laminated together, creating a kind of interior to the project.

Tightness is not defined by the scale of spaces but by how the project is positioned in the city. The house is adjoined on two sides, and the other two are within touching distance of neighbouring properties. It is literally and figuratively laminated into its surroundings, an idea best demonstrated through the sectional drawings produced to explain the project. The two exterior walls contain built-in joinery, air conditioners, bathrooms, circulation and other systems to support the operation of the dwelling.

This results in an interior that resembles the typical facade conditions found in Vietnamese cities - where a building's elevations become a platform for the accretion of services, equipment, and ad hoc additions. In this setting, *tightness* is less concerned with scale and more to do with an intensity of visual, formal or textural inhabitation.

New Office Works
Middleman
Hong Kong

New Office Works
Shortcuts
Hong Kong

This concept of saturation is very present at the urban scale of *super tight* cities. It is generated through urban environments and architecture adapting through processes of continual addition and accretion. Rather than absorbing change into a master plan, every alteration is a form of addition that adds an order, texture or pattern. It is a process that doesn't remove or correct but adds and accrues another layer. The delight of immediacy and expediency in this approach mirrors the daily life in mega-cities, both admired and derided.

Hong Kong is an artefact of the historical, social and economic forces that have shaped its growth. Hong Kong practice New Office Works describe the city through the concept of the *Middleman*, a series of films that explore the elements of the city's material culture.[1] The mercantile history of Hong Kong as a gateway port has left a rich and intricate trace in the fabric of the city. These documentary works suggest that a *tight* urban environment has not been subjected to constraint, removal or curation. Rather, the conditions allow for the operations of a city to be directly expressed in its form.

What is left is an assemblage that is surplus to Alberti's fifteenth-century description of beauty, being defined as 'a harmony of all the parts…fitted together with such proportion and connection, that nothing could be added, diminished or altered, but for the worse.'[2] By contrast, the *tight* city can be added to, altered, or have parts taken away with little impact on the overall legibility. The *super tight* city is a formal arrangement that achieves generosity, privileges multiple viewpoints and spatial readings over the single vision.

Each of these example projects suggest a formal language of density that has transcended social expectations, customs and functional requirements. Each project acquires its own autonomous cultural and spatial value within its setting.

Urban *tightness* is an artefact of the cultural rituals, social practices, economic and political circumstances of a given time. Yoshiharu Tsukamoto points to the emergence of micro urbanism and other *super tight* phenomena as the product of history.[3] However, as Tsukamoto has also identified, the shape and direction of our cities is not a foregone conclusion. We must be able to critically engage with and measure the qualities of our cities to decide on an appropriate direction for future development.

‘While showing the optimal possibility of living in a tiny space, at the same time we have to talk about the epic story of the twentieth century of Tokyo, for example. Because if you know that, you can imagine another future... another way to reconstruct the city.’[4]

To argue for *tightness*, it is necessary to detach the form and appearance of buildings and cities from the circumstances that produced them. We must begin to measure and understand *tightness* and define its formal and physical qualities beyond the footprint of human inhabitation. Designers need to develop a broader understanding of the formal consequences of density and continue to experiment through design speculation. Rather than assessing urban and architectural form through known functional templates, we must begin to identify formal qualities similar to those described above. These qualities can be understood independently of the circumstances from which they have emerged and are transferable. In a rapidly urbanising world, the formal language of the *super tight* city might be one prototype for sustainable growth.

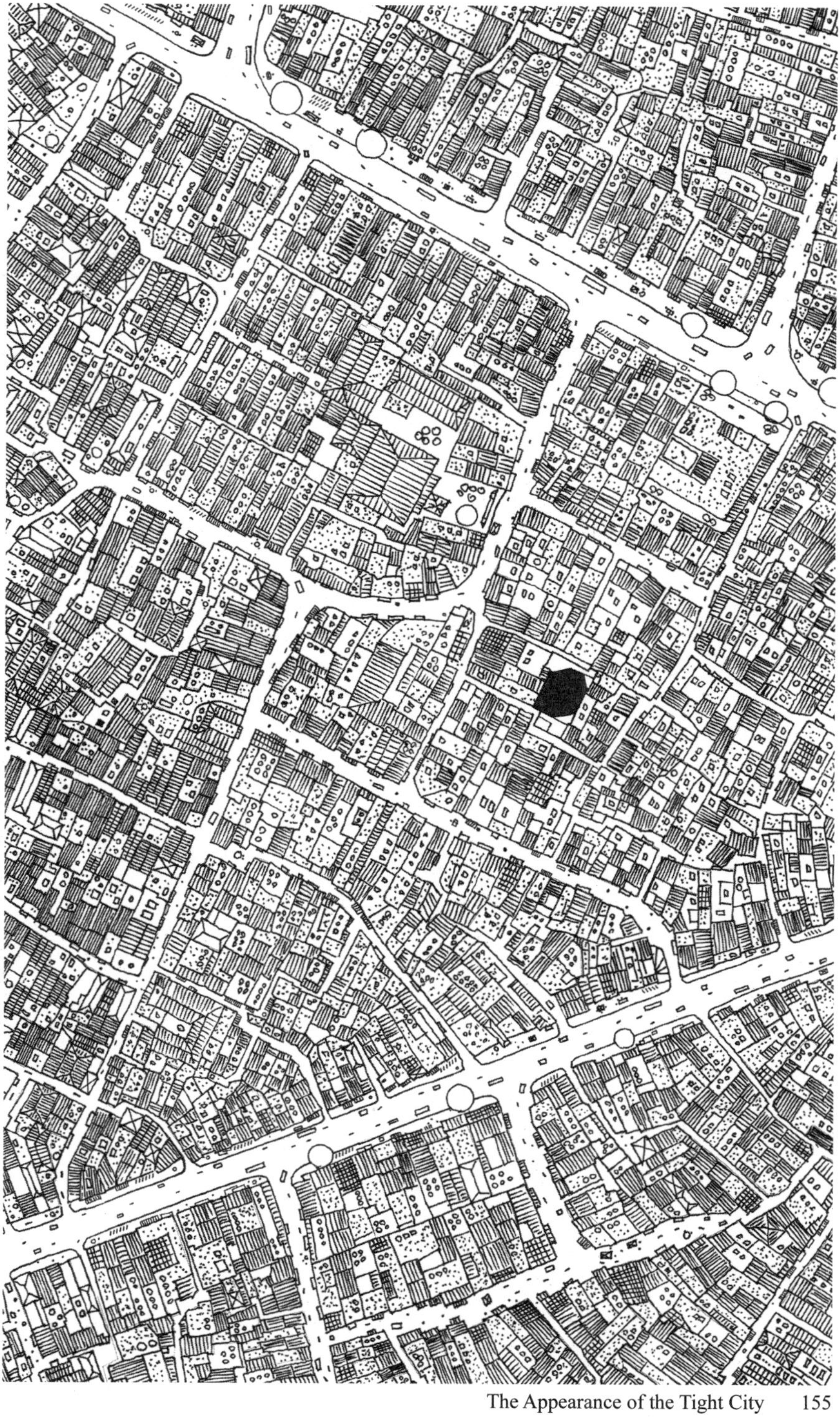

14

Tight Bar & Tight Hẻm

Architectural Installation

The Tight Bar and t*he Tight Hẻm* were full scale architectural installations made for the 2019 Super Tight exhibition and installed at the Design Hub gallery in Melbourne.

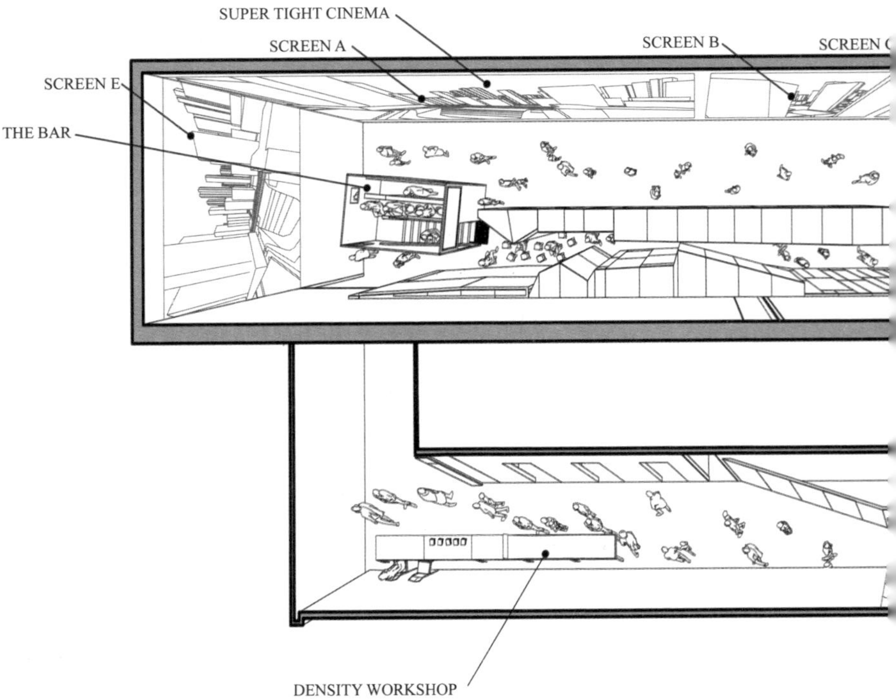
SUPER TIGHT CINEMA
SCREEN A
SCREEN B
SCREEN E
THE BAR
DENSITY WORKSHOP

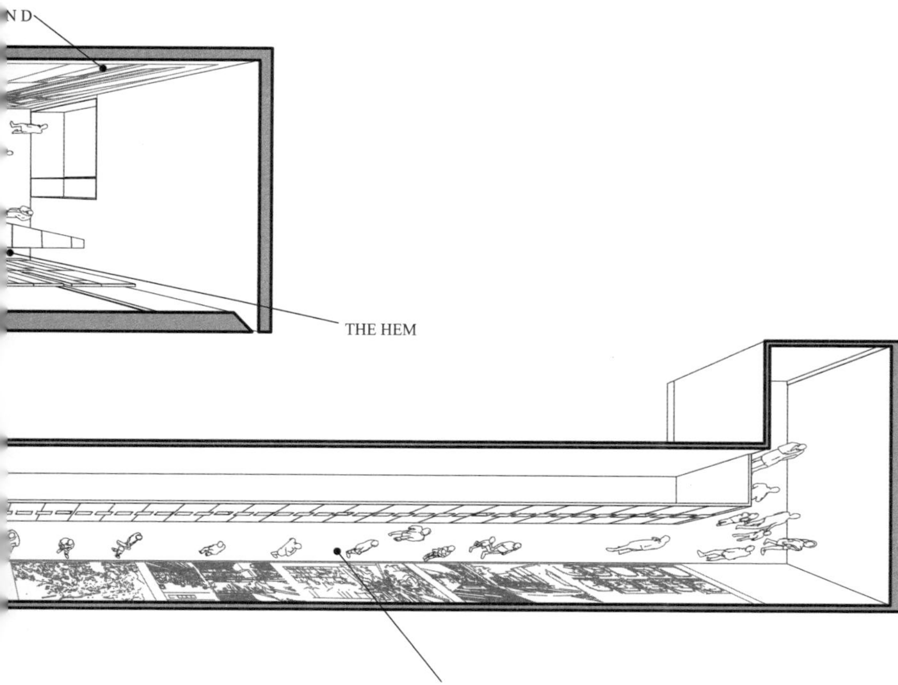
N D
THE HEM
SHIOZAKI LAB INSTALLATION

welcome

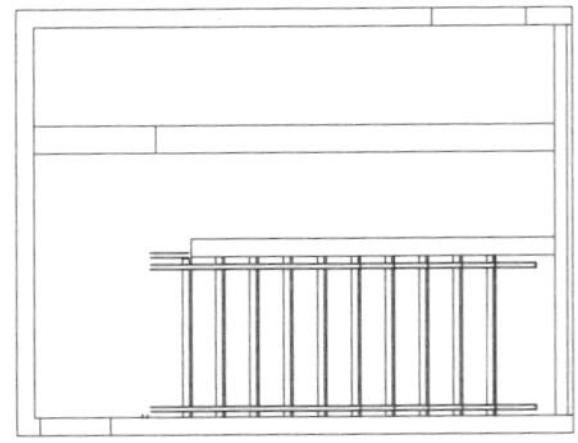

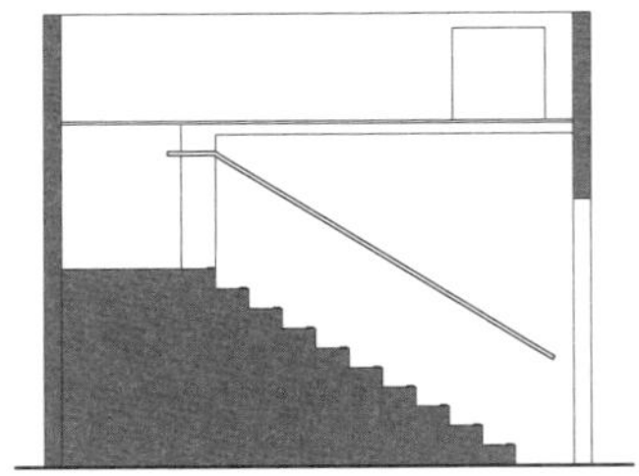

The Tight Bar, and indeed our use of the term *super tight*, draws its name from the bar in a Shibuya Yokocho just north of the train station. A favourite of John's while a student in Tokyo, it embodies both the generosity and the intensity of the urban *tight*. One absurdly little room elevated over a ground floor bar and accessed by a steep and narrow stair, it overlooks the rail lines north from Shibuya station. As the bar fills well beyond capacity, the stair becomes a stacked standing room. Getting a drink involves relaying an order to the bar via the those in front and for drinks to be passed across and over the stair's balustrade.

In the Super Tight exhibition, its transposition became not only a maquette at full size but the key venue for the series of talks within the event. Its composition within the gallery space made it the exaggerated, elevated stage for speakers and the most immersive location to view the *Tight Cinema* – a wall of large scaled projection works. Its composition with the *Tight Hẻm* object formed something of a tiny amphitheatre – the bar stair was set at the end of the *hẻm* so that the neck of its space faced the stair to the elevated bar.

The transposition of the *Tight Bar* into the gallery forced a radical shift. The demands of conventional inhabitation and its operation within the exhibition event created a process for abstracting the urban case study into the model object for exhibition. First, the stair needed to comply with the local building regulations. This stair length, in combination with the optimum height in the middle of the projection, set the height of the bar platform – a little lower than a full floor. The space below was enclosed (avoiding a separate fire compartment) and the space above was open (avoiding another fire compartment). This created an implied space, with the platform enclosed virtually.

Drinking and talking while seated at the timber bar is something between being on stage, being at a local drinking hole, and being the white plastic figure in an architectural model. Constructed in the same card as the *Hẻm*, it demonstrates without replication. Questions are forced into conversation by these two objects; being both stage sets and object on exhibition; a venue for the works, and participating in the works. What is the transferability of an urban model to another context? What is the level of abstraction required, and possible for an urban model to be meaningfully transposed? The conclusion is both spatial and provisional, entering a domain of setting general qualities for urban models which are at the same time highly specific to context. The conclusion is partly circumstantial but deliberately partial in its qualities. The particular form and geometry are critical to an urban model beyond its typical dimension or scale while the surface texture, detail and the ephemera of occupation remain particular to its original urban location, and beyond the scope of the case study model.

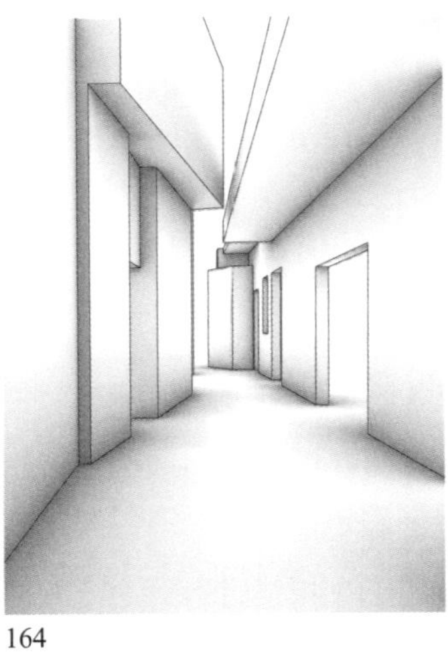
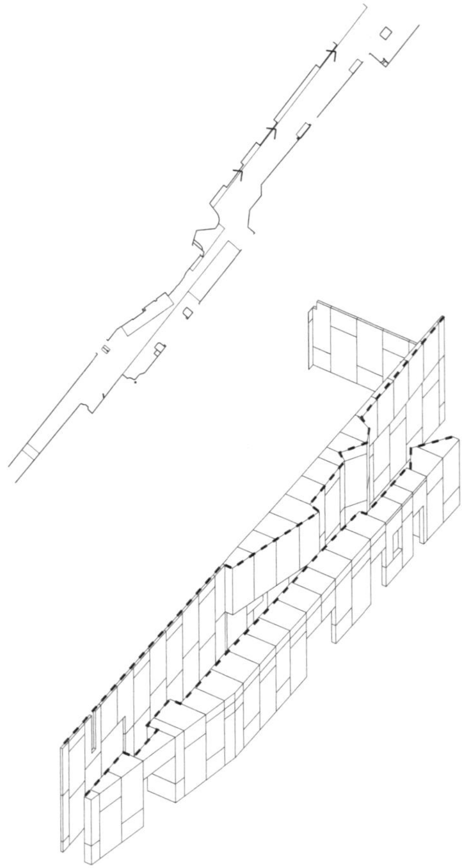

The Tight Hẻm installation, also made for the Super Tight exhibition, is a full size maquette of an urban space found in District 1 of Saigon. It was a venue to demonstrate the qualities and debate questions of the *supertight* city; ideas which are both discursive and experienced spatially. The spatial installation interacted with other works of the exhibition and with the volume of the gallery space; roughly halving it lengthwise and radically compressing its proportion. As an urban model it was a transposition, and an exercise in judging abstraction. The design of the piece asks: what is maintained, what is lost? What is preserved and specific: what is generalised in the abstraction? Urban models and their spaces often a search for a formula; quantifiable physical attributes which can be repeated or preserved. The ideal width of a street; the sectional proportions of a space, a set of ratios which create a quality. Yet which information is critical and which is dispensable?

First we identified a *hẻm*, a particular space unique in its location and specific form, yet one of hundreds in the city with comparable characteristics. This *hẻm*, a U shaped path which loops back to Pasteur street in the centre of District 1 is surrounded by luxury hotels, and increasingly global development. Narrow openings to the lane mask the second layer of the block structure - the network of tight and porous spaces. The space of these lanes are notable for four qualities: The compression of edges (a physical *tightness*); open and blurred edges (front rooms move in an out of the public realm daily); textured layered surfaces (its walls a gallery of scratched and stencilled messages), and the ad hoc geometry of its form. The first and last of these qualities are readily transposed and remain present in the *Tight Hẻm* object, repeatable and transferrable. The exercise in making the object (both 1:1 simulation and giant maquette) delineates between the transferrable and the site specific. The transposition proceeded with a mapping of the whole *hẻm*, and then identifying a fragment which would scale to the gallery space and form the object in a new context. As that fragment/object was modelled, a series of judgements were made on the ad hoc geometry; the kinks and crenulations formed by steps, ramps, canopies, and accreted constructions by countless unregulated adjustments. Its was critical not to iron out and flatten the geometry of the finely formed urban space, while also stepping away from a romance with texture and patina.

Finally the block was sliced – the *hẻm* object becoming a thickened stage set. Instead of its many openings leading into deep interiors, it opens vignettes into other parts of its gallery containers. The piece says little about the *hẻm's* rich occupation in Saigon. The Old Compass café; street vendors of juices and cigarettes; morning *pho* and afternoon television just a part of its life. The form as transposed though, is suggestive of occupation neither unique nor generic; not yet *tightened* through wear and use.

THANH
85 Pasteur, P.

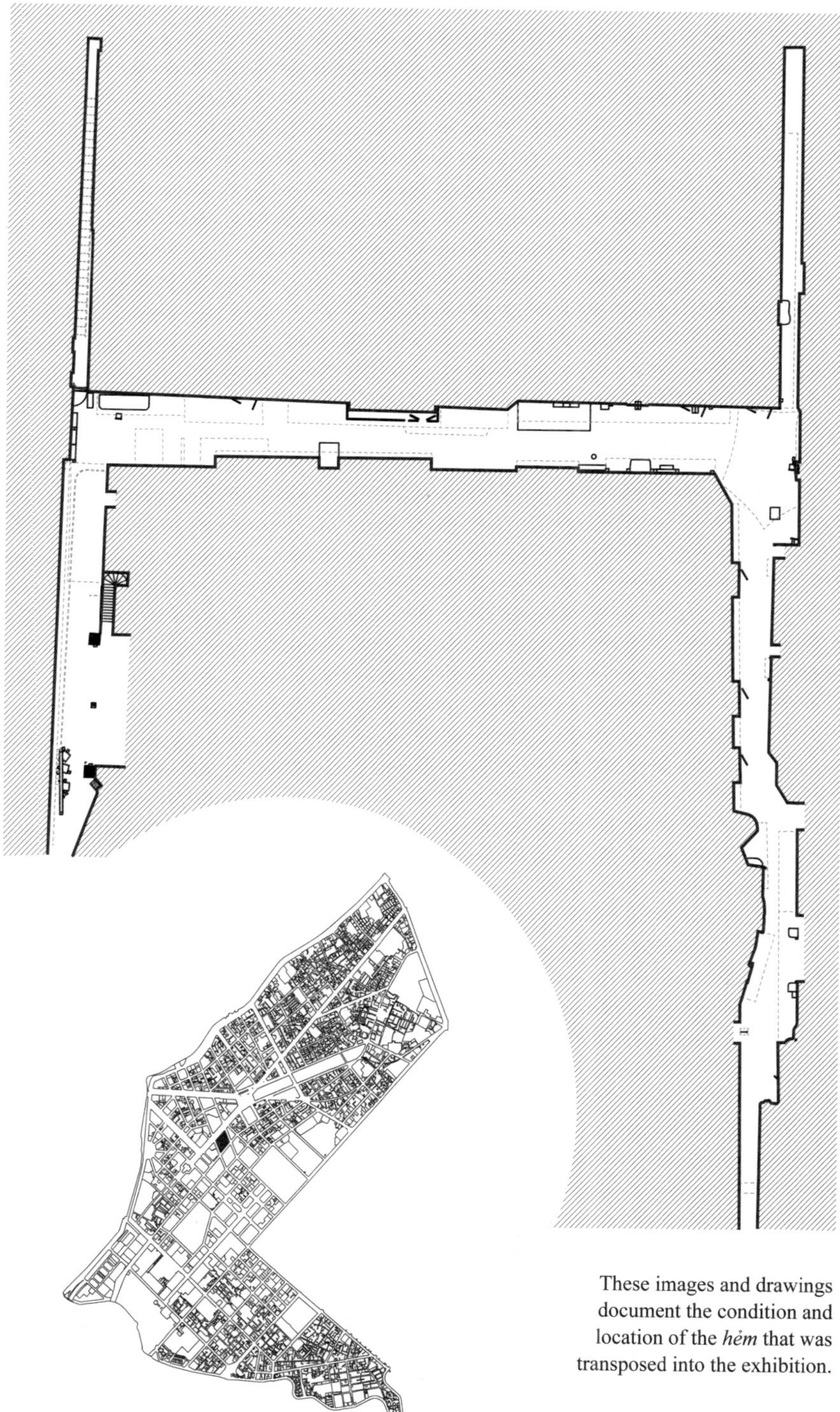

These images and drawings document the condition and location of the *hẻm* that was transposed into the exhibition.

The Tight Bar and *Tight Hẻm* under construction at the Design Hub Gallery in Melbourne 2019.

The Tight Hẻm activated for a series of public events and workshops in the Design Hub Gallery Melbourne 2019.

Van Cleef & Arpels
From the U.K.
シェーン
英会話
ENGLISH FOR LIFE
左隣ビル5F
中央コンタクト
MIDORIYA
川越ミドリヤ
質
大黒屋
Van Cleef & Arpels

15

An interview with architect Rafael A. Balboa, Tokyo

Rafael: My research focuses on urban and architectural teratology. Teratology is a branch of science that is concerned with embryology and deformations in the body. I have applied this as a metaphor to the city. More specifically, my doctoral dissertation was about prosthetic urbanism, which tries to understand buildings in the city as bodies. The objects that are added to the existing body are considered a prosthetic.

In my research, I have looked closely at the commercial areas of Tokyo – Shibuya, Shinjuku, Ueno, and Ginza. I was looking at all the elements that are added to the buildings in these areas over time. The work in the Super Tight exhibition was part of a catalogue of urban prosthetics in these areas, which ordered the different types and qualities of these prostheses.

John: Can you give us an example?

Rafael: Yes, the signboards are the perfect example because one of the things with urban prosthetics is that they often give identity to the building. To explain this, I like to use the analogy of Captain Hook. Captain Hook has an identity because of his hook. In the same way, urban prosthetics give identity to buildings. The signboards of Tokyo, for example, and in many Asian cities create a sense of identity for a building. At the same time, these aggregations are structured by the body, in this case, the building, and they supplement the host economically through additional revenue.

So, prosthetics are a supplement to the host. It's very different from a parasite. *Para* means besides, and *sitos* means to eat. So basically, the parasite establishes a detrimental relationship with the host. It's a negative relationship between the host and the parasite. The prosthetic supplements the body and enhances its original capabilities. In the same way, the signboards extend the functions of the buildings. You can tell what is happening inside, you can be attracted, you can draw profit, but at the same time, it provides a very strong identity.

Graham:	The prosthetic metaphor seems to align with the discussion we had previously about adjusting a city's form. If you think of the built fabric as the skeleton structure, all those additions are what enables the city to be *tightened* or to be tuned very finely.
Rafael:	It is true. It's a very flexible idea in this sense.
John:	The projects that you submitted are a catalogue of these cityscapes and forms of prostheses. Is there a particular one that is more representative?
Rafael:	In areas like Ginza, there are what we call 'crowns', older buildings that tend to receive more aggregations. These are not generic sign boards but made for each specific building. This was common practice between the 1970s up until the 1990s. It is a very particular trend that occurred in the city. In the newer buildings, the footprint is much larger, and these elements start to diminish. Basically, it is about communicating ownership. The more contemporary buildings have only one or two flagship stores, so they have fewer aggregations but are visually more prominent.
Graham:	You're saying that sites are agglomerating, therefore the number of owners is decreasing?
Rafael:	Correct. It is something we call land readjustment. The developer will try to buy many of these special buildings or smaller plots to fuse them together. If the site faces a wide street, the project can gain consent to build much higher. As a consequence, the city is densifying in the parts where you have long, wider streets. It is a completely different topology. In the past, there were multiple owners, but now there is only one.
Graham:	What you are describing is a trend in many cities – it's certainly a trend in Australia. It's a product of market-based land ownership. Tokyo is often used as an example of the opposite: it maintains tiny footprints because the land is divided over time rather than combined.

Rafael: That is correct. During the Edo period, there was the old city, or the lower city, which was completely cramped. There were a lot of very small houses in front of each other that had these micro identities in each community. It is completely different now.

Graham: Yes, and are there any steps being taken in Tokyo to limit or prevent land from being combined in this way?

Rafael: It is linked to who is making the city. Unfortunately, the majority of Tokyo is managed by the interest of real estate developers, so it is quite an inconsistent city. But this means that good pieces of architecture stand out.

John: In Tokyo, and other cities throughout Asia, there seems to be a tolerance for augmenting buildings without much concern for their identity. If you add signage to a heritage-listed piece of the urban fabric in Australia, it would be required to blend in with the existing.

Rafael: Yes, I realised there seem to be very few rules for all the signboards in Japan. There isn't any code or regulation. Actually, the only requirement is that you need to keep eighty centimetres of separation between buildings. So, we are talking about a very informal city. Its form is mutating precisely because of this informality. Once the building or body exists, all these iterative augmentations and prosthetics are not regulated by anyone.

John: I'm interested in the relationship between informality and sustainability. This conversation has played out in the context of an increasingly dire global climate outlook. Could you talk a little bit more about how informality is sustainable?

Rafael: Gordon Matta-Clark referred to the urban phenomenon as a 'profitopolis', which resonates with the spirit of a city like Tokyo. So, from an economic perspective, this informality is sustainable because it allows these places to survive.

John: Doesn't that also prolong a building's lifespan? Tokyo is an interesting place because the building lifespan is minimal – it has one of the lowest rates in the world. Melbourne is probably a little bit longer, but we tend to also knock down and rebuild things very quickly. Some of the most wasteful practices are internal refits and building refits through a change of use or expectation. Is it possible to minimise the amount of change that requires intensive capital works through processes like prosthesis and addition as a way of adapting and reusing? This would align economic sustainability with environmental sustainability.

Rafael: In Japan, fewer buildings are being demolished and replaced. People are more often retrofitting their buildings. More and more, we see the younger generation of architects in Japan completing renovations, which wasn't common in the past.

John: I think China will be the next country to really take that on.

Rafael: It could be. But I think China's economy is in a similar position as Japan in the 1970s. The GDP growth rate of China is currently about 6.7%, which was the same as Japan in the 1970s. So, I am sure many of these urban phenomena are also going to occur in China. But for now, I would expect this trend of replacing buildings to continue.

Graham: In your video works, you present parts of Tokyo in an extremely analytical way. The city appears very beautiful, but also very calm and orderly. It's an interesting counterargument to the prevailing idea that a hyperdense city like Tokyo is chaotic.

Rafael: This approach was based on J.F Geist's study of arcade typologies during the 1980s. In looking at these arcades, he documented and evaluated them in two-dimensional elevation. Obviously, this is manipulating the view, and we don't experience the city in this way, but it is very consistent and easy to make comparisons. All of the buildings are flat and at the same scale. You can understand these images as both a collective elevation and a cluster of individual specimens.

Graham: To me, it reads as surprisingly real, insofar as it doesn't read as a series of specimens. It is a piece of Tokyo.

John: It's not natural, but certainly very real.

Graham: They remind us of Ed Ruscha's collages of the Sunset Strip from the 1960s, where he would line up every building on a block and collage them together. The process is deliberately non-judgmental about the city: everything has equal status. There are no highlights or exceptions.

Rafael: Ruscha's collages were kind of flashy. For me, it's more about trying to capture the complexity of the city. Ruscha was more sentimental, more emotional. My work is very cold-blooded, it's trying to remove all the sounds and just put it in an intelligible way – it flattens the city.

And Tokyo can be seen as a high-resolution screen. So, the only way to understand the differences is to study each element at the smallest scale. We need to be very specific, pick one thing and understand it in detail. If you compare Ginza next to Shibuya or Shinjuku, they look so much alike. I think that it's only the nuances, which create the difference, and which allow you to understand the city.

アラビアンロック
ザ・ロックアップ
SMBC
CONSUMER
FINANCE
PROMISE
プロミス
エンタメ レストランタワー
SQUARE
北の家族
ロックアップ
ミステリアス
アラビアン
ロック
ウエディング パーティー 会議 レストラン ダーツ
旬鮮料理 オフ会 イベント 誕生会
レイク
PROMISE

Lu'82
SOLE
月の夢
5F
銀座カラー
渋谷109前店
居酒屋 千
3F
STLASSH
渋谷中央店
0円
駄菓子バー
平日 16時より
土日祝 15時より
SEASIDE
FamilyMart

16

0120-075-787
8F
7F
6F
ダーツバー
毎日翌朝5時まで営業中!
営業時間
11:00-23:00
2F
WASHIN
SALE
3冠受賞
永久返金保証
チャップアップ育毛剤

Ginza, Shibuya, Shinjuku Series

Rafael A. Balboa
(STUDIO WASABI ARCHITECTURE)
and Yasemin Sahiner

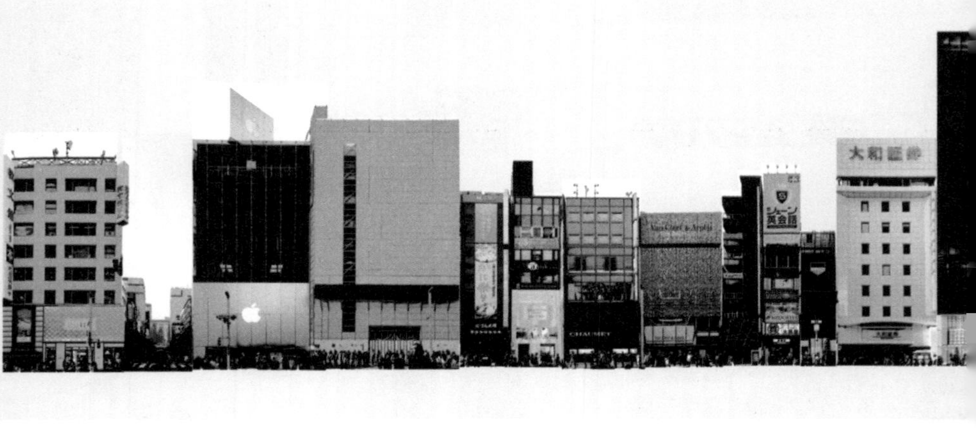

Cartier
MEIDI-YA

This series of images are a composite of multiple elevation photographs taken along major streets in the districts of Ginza, Shibuya and Shinjuku. The images attempt to cast an objective lens on the city, creating a constructed view in which the different streetscapes are presented in the same format and at a similar scale for the purposes of observation and comparison.

20-075-787
adidas
People!

Through this series, Rafael Balboa and Yasemin Sahiner are exploring and illustrating the notion of a prosthetic urbanism in Tokyo. Buildings in Tokyo, and many other Asian cities, are augmented through the addition of signs, billboards, graphics, LED screens and other systems that are not integral to the building. Often the building proper is smaller than the prosthetic, and the prosthetic takes on greater urban significance than the original structure. The series demonstrates the capacity for adaptation and augmentation in informal urban environments.

KAIUL
カイウル
SHIDAX

17

An interview with architects Paul Tse and Evelyn Ting from New Office Works

Paul: One of the main things that we are interested in is to connect our day-to-day environment, tradition and how things came to be the way they are. To bridge the past with the current requirements of contemporary society, especially in the context of Asian cities. Our contribution to the Super Tight project was our video series called *Middle Man Hong Kong*.

We grew up in Hong Kong. We were away for many years studying and working in practice. We gained more knowledge about architecture, forms of urbanism – particularly from western influences. Having studied in various places like Melbourne, the US and the UK, we were able to see the city in a new way. As soon as we returned to Hong Kong in 2017, we saw a lot of things that were very familiar to us but had a whole new level of meaning because of our training and practice overseas. The *Middle Man* video series allowed us to convey this fresh understanding.

Evelyn: Instead of just focusing on density, each episode of the *Middle Man* series explores small fragments of the architecture and urbanism. For example, there are episodes on shortcuts, palm trees, escalators, different types of urban objects or infrastructure – all of which demonstrate the city's response to urban density.

Graham: There is a really strong sense that this astonishing city, which is extraordinary to most people's eyes, is so much part of the everyday experience of its residents. So this sort of idea that *super tight* is just urban life for people in Hong Kong.

Evelyn: The towers become a backdrop to daily experience in the streets. We were interested in how people negotiate the extreme differences in terrain, how they access towers at different levels, and the kinds of interfaces between people and the city.

John: In Melbourne the public are very concerned with building height. Is that even an issue in Hong Kong?

Paul: Well, maybe not so much the height, but the size of units getting smaller and smaller is increasingly becoming a problem.

Evelyn: Another concern is how towers touch the ground, even between towers of relatively similar heights. The newer ones tend to plug into a podium that might be a shopping mall, whereas others might have a courtyard at the ground level, which provides a different experience.

Paul: Our video series is called *Middle Man* because we feel Hong Kong has historically always operated as an intermediary between the rest of the world and China. During the colonial era, if people from Europe and America wanted to produce goods from China, they would find a middle man in Hong Kong. This middle man would liaise between the west and the east.

This idea has permeated many aspects of Hong Kong's urbanism. For example, there are many surrounding mountains, and we have very little flat land. At the same time, there is a need to house a big population. As a consequence of these two extremes, we build on this mountain terrain and transport people and goods up and down through lift and escalator cores. We call these shortcuts – they connect the different levels of the city. So this is an example of how this characteristic urban mediation manifests in Hong Kong.

John: Design as an intermediary always results in strange circumstances or strange outcomes. It's not something an architect or an urban designer would design by choice, but it's quite good.

Paul: These kinds of conditions are almost like a quick fix. They are never well-planned or a well thought out result. In a sense, Hong Kong is very much a result of these layers of quick fixes.

Graham: It's such an interesting angle on seeing the whole of the fabric as somehow negotiated. When you're in the middle of it, it's habitable in a way that from the outside seems impossible.

John: What you have documented is a form of adaptation that is quite similar to the *rasquachismo* that Archie Pizzini has observed in Saigon. In your films, you identify this phenomenon at a bigger, more urban scale over a period of time. This condition suggests a cultural tolerance for adjustment and adaptation that probably would not be accepted in places like Melbourne, for example.

Paul: In Melbourne, and Australia in general, you still have the space to expand. Whereas Hong Kong is completely hemmed in by a small boundary, so we just have to deal with it. When we came back to Hong Kong, we felt that there was no architecture in the European or American sense. Everything is about pragmatism – about how you can utilise every single inch. But at the same time, there is a lot of construction, and 7.5 million people are living here. So we asked ourselves, is there another way of understanding architecture? Is there still room for architecture, and what can we learn from Hong Kong as an urban model?

Graham: I want to ask a question about *tightness* and poverty. There's been some discussion recently of people living in incredibly *tight* circumstances in big cities like Hong Kong and New York and so on, and the inequality of space. We're interested in uncoupling the idea of living small with concepts of poverty, and that conversely, wealth would immediately result in expanding out and living in a large apartment. Could there be an aspiration to choose a small footprint to live in, or is there always an aspiration to bust out of that?

Evelyn: I think there remains the aspiration to spread out. Space is equated with money. But those who are living in small spaces are forced to be more inventive in how things are put together and how a space is utilised. Space becomes more precious, and people are more careful in how they use it.

John: There is acculturation to density, which can result in perhaps undesirable circumstances like the subdivided apartments in Hong Kong. However, it is interesting to see how different circumstances can produce radically different perceptions of acceptable density.

Paul: Perhaps as an alternative, Tokyo is a very good example of how you can have high levels of density, but at the same time, people still live in individual detached houses. That never happens in Hong Kong except for billionaires.

Evelyn: Hong Kong is dominated by a single housing typology. Whereas in other parts of south-east Asia, like Singapore, you find high-density urban conditions alongside different kinds of housing typologies.

John: In Melbourne, many developers are marketing small footprint living at the upper end of the housing market. The key to this is the location of the units – in places like Fitzroy, which have extremely high levels of amenity. The city then becomes more important than the apartment itself.

Paul: Similarly, in Hong Kong, the school network also determines the price of real estate. Also, the kind of transportation and proximity to your employment. That cost is on top of the actual domestic space.

John: Architects could potentially be middle people. Other disciplines are either too close to the design or too far removed. The architect has a unique middle position – they can design these spaces while understanding them as integral to these networks you have identified in the *Middle Man* films.

Paul: I think this is true. Hopefully, we can connect the living spaces, the actual physical spaces of architecture, to ideas that operate beyond architecture – to social, cultural and urban issues.

Evelyn: It can be challenging to link larger urban cultural and political issues with private interior work. So we hope that in the future we have more opportunities to work on public projects.

18

Middleman, Shortcuts, Palm Tree

Paul Tse & Evelyn Ting
New Office Works

The *Middleman* series of films explores the urban environment of Hong Kong, its historical formation and contemporary condition through the lens of architecture, urban formations and material.

New Office Works describe Hong Kong as a 'middleman', a city that emerged as a global trading capital, and the intermediary between China and the west. Their films explore how the city has emerged through a series of processes, circumstances and negotiations.

Despite its density, a large percentage of Hong Kong's territory is designated as parkland, forest and greenspace. Middleman Episode 4 "*Palm Trees*" describes the manufactured nature of Hong Kong's seemingly natural tropical landscape, best represented through the ubiquitous palm tree. Prior to colonisation, the island was largely barren. As the city grew, the island and the expanded territories were artificially vegetated, through largely introduced species of palm (and other) trees. Contrary to the notion of a growing city encroaching on existing greenery, the greening of the city was integral to the process of urbanisation.

Much of Hong Kong is built on steep and mountainous terrain. To be able to move people efficiently from different levels of the city a series of 'shortcuts' have been created. This includes stairs, lifts, ramps, escalators and travelators, which allow pedestrians to move up the terraced slopes of the city.

中華基督教會灣仔堂
FULL
AVIS

These shortcuts are often hybridised with public and private buildings, and illustrate processes through which the city has adapted itself to accomodate the dense occupation of its territory.

19

An interview with Vietnam-based, Japanese architect Sanuki Daisuke

Graham: Your works are a great example of working in an extremely dense environment. What does the term *super tight* mean to you?

Sanuki: We were working on a model project in Hanoi focused on high density – about 3000 people per hectare. We were very concerned with how to improve the quality of that density in developing cities. Hanoi was a city where it was easy to knock things down very quickly; I would travel around the city and say, wow, that's disappeared already. So, the city was rapidly changing. Tokyo is an example of density being created little by little. So it is potentially easy to make high-density cities in Vietnam. A large rural population has moved into cities like Hanoi and Ho Chi Minh City. As a consequence, the population has quickly grown.

Our *Nga house* in District 10 is an interesting reference for this growth. The client's mother had been living in the same house for 40 years. When they moved into the area, there was very little. That area has no urban design, no planning strategy, but it has some unique qualities and shapes to the lanes.

Graham: We've had discussions around the differences between Tokyo and Ho Chi Minh City in terms of the way people manage the density and *tight* space. You have a unique position of living and working in both those places.

Sanuki: Tokyo is a city with very *tight* spaces. You witness what we call *super tight events*, like what happens on the trains. But in fact, the city is very large. If we focus on the buildings that have one metre spaces between them, it's not that dense. In Vietnam, there is no regulation for joining buildings, so they are tightly joined together. It seems much denser. There is a different feeling in Tokyo between people and how land is used. For instance, every building has to be set back 500mm from the boundary line, so there is a metre corridor between buildings. It is a Japanese law that creates a buffer area and contributes to the small building footprints.

These buildings are often 30 sqm, whereas, in Vietnam, it is generally around 100 sqm. Buildings, therefore, become larger when they don't have this gap and are joined on the boundary. In Tokyo, people often want a special house project – sometimes a crazy house project. In a tiny area, architects will try a strong idea that is challenging. In Vietnam, it is different – clients don't like to have a crazy house. When I started working in Vietnam, I noticed that clients were interested in the house being spacious. They did not appreciate a 2m x 2m bedroom, for example. They have *tight* urban places, but their attitudes are a little different for their domestic spaces. I often ask, what makes a rich house? In Tokyo, the *tight* and complex context creates interesting housing designs that, in turn, create happiness and a rich life.

Graham: Apart from the house and home, there is, for example, a strong café culture in Saigon. Do you think this affects the *tightness* of the city?

Sanuki: Ho Chi Minh City and Hanoi have a great deal of outdoor activity. A café extends outside more easily than in a city like Tokyo. In Vietnam, they are more flexible and less strict. An umbrella or an awning can create shade to allow for a table and some chairs. Vietnam's streets are, therefore, very full. On the other hand, Tokyo is about staying warm inside.

Graham: Yes, that has a strong effect on how that city reads. Yet, in your projects, there is often a private courtyard. Is that unusual in the Vietnamese context?

Sanuki: In dense cities like Ho Chi Minh City, I try to make the house into a hub. We have to focus not on building but on creating space which is important for the tropics. This is my strategy for an urban house – to create a space, a void. It allows for daylight, airflow and greenery. We often connect the private rooms with a courtyard. In dense cities, courtyards or voids within the plan are valuable.

Graham: It is a luxury in a very dense city and quite an unusual type in the Saigon context.

It is more common to open onto the *hẻm*, whereas this sets up an interesting relationship.

Sanuki: Our office always has a project in the *hẻms*, as a large percentage of Ho Chi Minh City's housing is located in *hẻms*. We have four residential types here in Vietnam: the villa, the townhouse, the rooming apartment and the rural house. Type two, the townhouse type, is around 80% of the residential buildings in urban areas of Vietnam. As a result of this building type, there is a rich street and public life.

Graham: So the courtyard is a response to that outdoor lifestyle, but secure and private? *Tightened*?

Sanuki: Yes, a solution with a lot of voids. It creates a grand, outdoor hallway to a small room. Clients want to make at least four or five bedrooms in a small house. These spaces can become dark and humid, so we make an open void.

Graham: These houses have many bedrooms. Are these for big families?

Sanuki: No, only three people, but sometimes they have family members who stay with them from the rural areas. There is always room – like a resort hotel guest room.

Graham: I want to ask a more detailed question relating to the outer skin on your projects. In previous projects, you have used terracotta breeze blocks to create a thick outer skin. However, for the *Hem House*, there is a subtle steel grille over the windows that creates a filtered view of the city.

Sanuki: In the *Hem House*, we tried to make a pattern in steel. In the southwest wall, it has a thickness of about four centimetres. So when people outside walk past, they cannot see inside. The house is in a very *tight* area, so we had to solve these privacy and security problems. We needed steel grille bars, but not like a jail. We translated Vietnamese motifs for the steel pattern and set them outside. We gave extra depth to the steel to increase privacy. These types of materials and ideas are important in the urban context.

20

Ho Chi Minh City House Series

Sanuki Daisuke Architects

Sanuki Daisuke is a Japanese architect working in Ho Chi Minh City. In a remarkable series of houses in that city, he has explored the possibilities of the home in the very dense environment of Ho Chi Minh City's neighbourhoods; adapting certain sensibilities from Japan through a rigorous view of tropical and *tight* urban situations. The body work has encompassed his arrival in Vietnam in 2009 as an urban researcher with the Kojima Kazuhiro laboratory, and his key contributions to the practice of Vo Trong Nghia as a partner in the VTN office. The work continues independently through Sanuki Daisuke Architects, where these projects are exemplars of living in this *tight* city.

The Binh Thanh Apartments are squeezed into a site down a lane in a fast developing district of the city – a fact only fully revealed by the drone video or view from a tower. The tightly packed, fine grained precinct faces a major expressway and tunnel, with an enormous high rise development opposite. It is these towers that give the view of the façade as an object. At street level the terracotta screens are perceived obliquely. The screen conceals a carefully figured narrow courtyard, giving great generosity to its six small apartments.

The Hẻm House negotiates its tight circumstances through the creation of an apparent thickness to its skin. The reveals of windows, coupled with a delicate metal grille which has enough depth so that obliquely the interface with its super close surroundings are screened. This buffer is amplified by the depth of joinery around the perimeter of the space – an effect which is continued on to the heavily screened roof garden. The effect is a remarkably filtered relationship with its extremely dense surroundings.

The NGA house continues SDA's hybridisation of *hẻm* types and courtyard dwellings. The building is almost invisible in its surrounds at street level, embedded in a web of narrow lanes and a sea of packed buildings of varying scales. The walled courtyards and cuts into the mass of the form give the interior an extraordinary generosity and an intimate relationship with both private gardens and the *tight* city around it.

SUPER
TIGHT
SUPER

21

Situation and Desire in the Tight City

Is a very high density city desirable in itself? Does a high density city exist simply in response to economic and political circumstances and situations or also after the desires of its inhabitants? Is it merely a by-product of a measurable after-effect or is it a quality of a city? If urban density is usually an outcome of external circumstances, could it occur without them? Could density be the outcome of a social desire? We use the term *tight* to loosely describe the coalescence of physical density and close social organisation. It might flip the terms in which we typically think about density and make it the object of desire without a necessary foreseeable limit.

We contend that high density, and urban dispersal for that matter, are generally seen as the natural result of external material forces and that the task of urban planning has been to control and limit density. More recently, even when the city planner's role has been to control sprawl and consolidate sustainably, it is within an framework of a limit. That limit is a response to the dangers of the hyperdense or overcrowded cities witnessed in the previous centuries. It is a logic built into twentieth-century design which continues to linger. But can this logic be reversed? Could the *tight* city be constructed on the desire for minimums rather than maximums? Could the aim of planning be to facilitate density rather than control it? Could urban planning conceive of minimum density, its role being to satisfy the desires for closeness and compact living?

Very dense cities are usually seen as the convergence of material circumstances. The study, *Lessons from Europe's Densest Neighbourhoods*, identifies the highest density neighbourhood in each European nation and ranks them for inhabited density.[1] It suggests nearly all of the continent's densest urban quarters were constructed from 1850 to 1914. A convergence of three circumstances formed these nineteenth-century hyper-dense cities. Firstly, rapid industrialisation brought large urbanising working populations together. New developments in construction technologies, such as elevators and concrete frames, allowed for taller buildings. And finally, walking was still a necessity in these city centres. Walking from your home to a place of work was a recipe for a dense city. Almost no urban environments constructed after World War One have achieved the density of that period, with many reducing in density since that time. Most of these neighbourhoods were described as undesirable when first constructed, however, many have since become desirable through gentrification. Of the neighbourhoods ranked, those in Barcelona and Paris were the densest by a significant measure. Global tourists and new urbanists alike might also agree that these two are among the most desirable cities on earth.

Conversations on great cities often get stuck on the proposition that they are desirable but not replicable. Conversely, cities like Paris and Barcelona are considered the template for future urban density. Rapidly changing Asian cities are significant in overcoming fixed or historical images of the hyperdense city as they have experienced explosive growth more recently and produced a variety of responses. For instance, the urban subdivision of Tokyo, driven by inheritance taxes, has resulted in the emergence of a generation of micro-scaled villas. Similarly, the historical taxation of street width in Vietnam, combined with rapid urbanisation, has resulted in the tube house typologies. These brief examples reveal how the historical circumstances contribute to urban by-products.

In considering the gentrified nineteenth-century city, untangling the distinction between desire and circumstance may no longer be necessary. It may no longer be relevant to ask what causes very dense urban environments? It might be practical to ask which kind of urban environments, which now exist, are the most desirable? More importantly, are cities less desirable as a result of being denser? And how does this compare with the desirability of low-density cities?

The contradictions of hyperdensity, both excess value and lack of resources, converge to create the perception that a place is out of control. The two contrasting images of Manhattan and Mumbai serve as a diagram of this phenomenon. The dispersed city is healthy, giving space to sanitation and overcoming the epidemic diseases of proximity. Facilitating the infrastructures of sanitation but also managing the moral problems of overcrowded working classes became a preoccupation of modern planning.

Density often grows from uncontrolled capital speculation. The profit motive drives high-rise development, reducing space to a minimum to accommodate expanding land value and construction prices. However, density also grows from conditions of poverty like those documented in Mumbai slums or Lower East Side tenements. This condition is the flip side of capital speculation: maximising space while responding to scarcity. Both circumstances share the qualities of being uncontrolled and unplanned. Both are circumstantial rather than desirable: the scarcity of space masks the desirability of the tight environment.

The two basic metrics for urban density, inhabitants per square metre and overall building volume, are often conflated in research on cities. In recent centuries, urbanisation has seen the size of the individual private house and the population footprint rapidly increase. Ho Chi Minh City's dense core, District 1, is an example of the effects of urbanisation on density and building volume. In this case, the nineteenth-century urban fabric is now contained in a low-rise envelope with a low square metre rate per person. The three to five-storey buildings commonly found in District 1 are some of the densest in the world. As the explosive growth in the city's economy redevelops this area into a business district, the built volume increases and the population per area diminishes. The way this area is also used changes as office and retail space displace housing. Like many other rapidly modernising cities, this increase in high-rise development is also accompanied by growth at its perimeter.

Twenty-first-century technology has contributed to a culture of miniaturisation in modern devices and electronics. In architectural programs and space, it can influence a reduction in a city's urban footprint. Automated deliveries, ride-sharing in autonomous vehicles, urban agricultural techniques, virtual communications, home 3D printing are some of the technologies that both disrupt and streamline a city's spaces. Each has the potential to compress the footprint of a city and to create greater human density. As the vast floor areas of factories, supermarkets, office spaces and car parks become redundant, their urban built volume and the infrastructure that supports them also evaporates.

This image of a highly tuned, miniaturised technology is desirable. Our interest in urban density and use of the term *tight* relates less to the efficiencies of technology and more to the creation of social bonds through urban proximity. The relationship between how we measure the physical density of a city and its social *tightness* is complex. Social bonds are widely viewed as a desirable quality in cities. Proximity is a precondition for a socially desirable settlement: even affluent suburban properties are described through access to a social network. All cities, even low-density cities, are defined by proximity and a series of desirable connections. The technologies that could bring us physically closer together might recast our sense of a maximum density and eliminate the objects that stand between us. Some of those objects include redundant spaces of cities and planning controls; spaces made redundant by new forms of transport and manufacture, and planning controls which no longer need to separate them. With these constraints removed, we could assume that a tighter city is desirable, and that urban planning controls need not artificially thwart that condensing.

Barcelona 1930

Manhattan and Mumbai, each consquences of the circumstance of scarcity

Archie Pizzini Rasquachismo Series, Vietnam

Another persisting dream of modern technology is the belief that it will bring social liberation through access, and as a consequence, it might overcome class systems or disadvantages. This belief is coupled with the idea that the resulting liberation will strengthen social bonds. Yet affluence remains the driver of a dilated and expanding urban footprint common to western cities. Greater affluence usually corresponds to a larger physical footprint and separation. Economically equal societies are shown to be more socially cohesive.[2] The complicated relationship between the socially *tight* and the physically *tight* is nevertheless crucial. The task of the *tight* city is decoupling density from poverty, scarcity, exclusion and conformity. This task is connected to technology and is already observable in the world's *tight* cities. Successfully living in *tight* environments can shape behaviours and desires. The existing examples of dense cities are as powerful a measure as much as planning policy or advocacy.

The existence of cities is qualitative evidence of the value of density. They prove what density looks and feels like in its variations. They are the concrete intersection of desire and circumstance and evidence of density beyond what is ever planned. The *tight* city as-found often exceeds the planned or projected city in the intensity of its occupation. The images of *tight* cities alongside this essay are qualitative observations, evidence of their circumstances, and projections of a desirable city.

The photographic images of Ho Chi Minh City by Archie Pizzini and Sue Hajdu are documentary records infused with nostalgia and romance. Each image captures the qualities of closeness and intimacy in Vietnamese cities and the ingenuity and care in using or shaping the urban environment by its inhabitants. Both photographers capture the intense but subtle adjustment of the physical surroundings. They are witness to the transformation of Vietnam's urban environment since the 1990s and assert the value of an urban culture that is well adapted to its *tight* footprint. Desiree Grunewald, a collage illustrator working in the same city, makes real fiction from Ho Chi Minh City's alleys. Here, the montage works compress urban space literally, by overlapping its photographed material. But the montaging eye of Grunewald has identified this *tight* urban environment as already full of moments of visual overlapping, elision and occlusion. They are already a montage, sometimes indistinguishable from the cut up version. For Andrew Stiff, the medium of film for observing these same environments is an act of abstracting and amplifying the qualities of visual and occupied density.[3] The filters of blurring, of *tightening* the frame, of layering serve to heighten the allure of the everyday and close-up life of Ho Chi Minh City's streets. What Andrew Stiff calls the creative archive is both a desired recording of the real and a tool of advocating for the city he records.

Sue Hajdu
Urban Documentation
Vietnam Series

Desirée Grunewald
Habitats Series
Vietnam

Andrew Stiff
Hẻm Series
Vietnam

This collection of visual observations stares unflinchingly at the city but often also, in a dreaming and nostalgic manner. There is an assertion, through the depictions, that what exists in the famously wild city is not chaos but a highly considered and networked orderliness.

The Shiozaki Laboratory drawings of Tokyo stand at the junction of circumstance and desire.[4] This is evident in how these works refuse to differentiate between the analytical and narrative linework. The scenes depicting Tokyo show their inhabitants contending with everyday life while pursuing the pleasures and freedoms of close sociability. The cherry blossom festival crowds are alongside the daily commuter crush, and indeed all functions of the city are set alongside each other, sometimes incongruously, sometimes overlapping seamlessly. The least desirable of these, the train carriage, is also the most monofunctional and a direct consequence of the segregation and dispersal of urban life. The city Shiozaki describes is shaped by a set of behaviours that temper desires and channel them toward a collective negotiation with *tight* living. Tohru Horiguchi's film of the Bingo House in Osaka takes a particular circumstance, the absence of chairs, as a subtle spatial disruption and act of *tightening*. These scenes appear like an experiment to test behavioural effects. In response to this film, we can ask what can be gained through omission and encouraging this kind of density?

The Diamond Village series by Drawing Architecture Studio is part of a body of work that tackles the full intensity and complexity of the *tight* city, in this case, Shenzhen, through line drawing both fantastic and forensic. Simultaneously capturing the city as an object and observing individuals in the dense maze, the drawing is above, below, inside and outside these spaces. The effect is dizzying and fantastic. Yet the drawings accurately transpose the lively, peripheral and less planned piece of Shenzhen. The drawing style is crucial. It depicts a saturated and full urban environment, rendered as a benign, cartoon video game. It is an aesthetic of the busy, saturated and lively. Unlike the often evacuated and dystopian visions of Archigram, Superstudio or the Metabolists, the future in Diamond Village is teeming and populated. It is a transposition from situations to desire. It is this condition: the full embrace of the situations and circumstances compressing cities that is present in all of the fictionalised depictions and studied observations of super *tight* cities.

Tohru Horiguchi
Bingo House (video still)
Osaka

Shiozaki Lab
Hanami (detail)
Tokyo

Drawing Architecture Studio
Diamond Village (detail)
Shenzhen

The conditions for very dense cities in the nineteenth-century exist in a different way today. The environmental case for a *tight* footprint is compelling, yet it requires us to make a choice and reverse common practices. Desire can co-opt that choice and overcome its resistance. We could imagine that the discipline of urban planning might take on new tasks and a new set of aims. We could frame this as the third stage or era for the centuries-old project of urban design. The first of these stages saw the city made for protection, the walled fortress. Secondly, the city made for health, the zoned and dispersed systems of the twentieth century. These include modernist projects such as *Ville Radieuse* or the Garden City. And finally, the city as a tight system or network. The conditions for the tight city are transformative. The problems traditionally associated with crowded cities have mostly disappeared with post-industrial sanitation and medicine. The contemporary city suffers from isolation, as much as from overcrowding.

The imperatives to *tighten* our carbon footprint have reversed the paradigm of limiting density and facilitating dispersal. The role of *tight* urban planning in this imagined third era is to facilitate hyper-density, to reconcile the impulses of the previous two eras and to capture new techniques of compressing urban programs. It is not to formulate a blueprint for new cities or justifications for erasure but to adjust, recast and backfill existing urban settings. For this era, extreme density is a natural desire, and it is not the task of urban planning to thwart it. Making a case for super compact or dense cities is pointless unless it is coupled with desire. If high density is seen purely as the consequence of scarcity, whether that scarcity means poverty or extreme land values, then it continues to be something to manage, control or limit. Images of density are stereotyped by overcrowded people or overcrowded architecture. Perhaps the image of *tightness* should be the crowded bar, the street festival, the teaming market – the image of celebrating closeness in events and everyday life. The point of the term *super tight* is to inject desire into the problem of the urban footprint.

f the bui
ilding c

22

A conversation with Luke Thornton, Beulah International and Aaron Roberts, Edition Office

John: Luke, can you begin the discussion on property development by talking through your role in procuring buildings and some of the issues you have faced over the last couple of years.

Luke: Beulah's Melbourne property development projects are often small scale buildings with large footprint apartments targeted at owner-occupiers such as young families, down-sizers and empty nesters. These projects let us explore ideas in architecture, design and livability. *Southbank by Beulah* is a project, currently in planning of 227,000 square metres. It is a mixture of residential, hotel, commercial, retail, entertainment spaces, cultural spaces, and extensive landscaping.

Graham: One of the issues that led to the Super Tight project was the discourse around development and the anxiety about density that seems to exist in this city. The kind of projects you're describing have probably done a lot to overcome that anxiety – due to design and delivery quality. Yet, the anxiety about density does persist. We're interested in how you prise apart high-density development and its negative connotations.

Luke: We are conscious of those anxieties, and we anticipate them as a project comes to life. We anticipate these conversations with our Southbank project. We've travelled the world with our architects at the start of the design process – from New York, London, Tokyo, Bangkok, Singapore – to observe the best examples of mix-use, high-density development. We found that most high-density projects are often over transport hubs – a strategy that is in everybody's interest. Southbank is very close to transport, but we're not over a train station.The benefit of living in a high-density urban environment is the proximity to the activities that we love: dining out, entertainment and being close to our workplace. It is being close to the places where we spend our free time, without the constraints and isolating down-times of commuting and traffic.

We see that as a mindset to promote, one that is prevalent in Asia and cities like New York and London. Yet here in Australia, this idea is still in development. We see it as a real opportunity: proximity to things is a luxury.

John: The case has been made in Southbank. It is already pretty dense in units per square kilometre. In places like Doncaster, or middle ring suburbs, these ideas are a significant increase in density. Do you have a prepared argument for these areas? Or is it something that you deal with on a case by case basis?

Luke: These concerns need to be addressed on a case by case basis. The biggest argument is made by the people who complete the first project in an area. These developments need to occur near employment, education and transport hubs. We haven't ventured into areas with limited development. We would only have that conversation if the supporting drivers, like transport and employment, were already in place.

John: We've spoken a lot during this project about the notion of a model. The idea that architects and developers can make new models for high-density living.

Aaron: I don't think we have found the solution, but I can talk about some of the challenges our office has faced, and the questions we have for developers. To begin on procurement and the financial models, you could argue that in the last 20 years, buildings have been shaped – the way they look, the program and everything – by the financial models that underpin them. Some of the requirements of contemporary living are not being addressed by models motivated by financial gains and market forces. In our experience with multi-res development, there is a lot of pressure placed on the results required by those financial models. We've attempted to challenge the layout or what kind of family unit could move into these developments, but it's difficult to overcome the constraints inherent to the model. For instance, we might go to council with a spread of single-bed, two-bed and three-bed apartments in the development.

These are apartments that families could move into; apartments for downsizers. We get through the council, but then the layouts are altered by going to market – the internal plans are completely adjusted.
We've also been seeing other interesting models such as rent to build scenarios, the Baugruppen model or Nightingale. I am interested to know if developer's want to challenge existing financial models to create more diversity within a development.

Luke: Yes, the way you structure finance often dictates the way you design. In New York, we found the model is completely different. For developers of high-quality projects, it's not uncommon to complete the project with very few sales. If they can sell that project out within a year of completing it, that is a big success. So in New York, the financiers will fund a good project to make it happen. That is very different from Australia. Here you have to design a project to get pre-sales. For this, you need a range of products, and you need a range of price points so you can make enough early sales to get banks to finance you.

Graham: What we're suggesting here is that the banking sector has as much to do with the way that our cities look as any other factor.

Aaron: Oliver Wainwright spoke about this recently. Residential markets are now one of the largest sectors of currency relative to investment in the world. This is having massive impacts on the makeup of housing and cities.

John: I'm interested in the differences between New York and cities in Australia. That housing is sold once complete is unique for our setting. If you're selling a space that people can walk through, that is particularly appealing from a design perspective. You have the opportunity to demonstrate the value of design in the intended medium at the point of sale.

Graham: Could that be put down to what we might call maturity of the market? Building property in Manhattan is bankable to a degree, whereas Southbank is still considered uncertain. It's the maturity of both the urban fabric and the financial institutions that fund housing.

Luke: Yes. New York's market is unique: it has a handful of developers and a handful of financiers. This group has completed maybe half of all developments in that city, which means that they have the security of other projects to support their debt. But it is also a mindset. For instance, they're shocked by the level of pre-sales that we need to achieve to start construction. They say, 'Just build it. Build a good product.'

Aaron: I've often noticed that everything is on the line to get the pre-sale. For instance, an entire internal layout can be reworked to complete a sale. Sometimes this process can lead to good outcomes, sometimes not.

John: We're talking about a particular section of the market. The apartment industry is relatively new in Melbourne and Australia. There are great examples of high-density living from the early twentieth century, but this scale of development is a recent phenomenon. So, it is still finding its way. This includes both how we describe high-density living and the methods of finance. So, what is the difference between pitching to a high-end market and pitching to the other half? Can you speculate on what is particular to these groups? And is it harder or easier?

Aaron: We have completed projects across different areas of the market. For instance, we have built more affordable townhouse models where the quality and the level of sale hasn't been different to more high-end options. We find that people are looking for different types of housing. We are also interested in financial models that tailor the end product for the people that will occupy it. This is partly a response to the affordability issue. Of course, the land value in the city is much higher, so how do you create models where you can have more people moving into the city?

One solution is increasing height and density limits. But how do you get the existing model to work for high-end apartment living and, at the same time, fuel densification?

Luke: Land value is always the business foundation of property development. It doesn't matter what sector you're working in: whether it's the most affordable or the very top-end of the market, the product always has to represent value for money to the purchaser. At the high-end of the market, you're competing against an architect commission to design a custom house.

We offer good design by appointing an architect and managing the build ourselves. So, for a purchaser, it comes down to a custom home or a very nice apartment. At the other end, where affordability is important, it's about creating a good product with benefits and attributes for an accessible selling price. That is the simple equation. In our Southbank project, we have all of those price points and the benefits. A third element is mixed-use and proximity to retail and food. Even office space within a development adds value. So, combining different land uses within the same block or same development increases purchase value.

Graham: This is a nice segue into the idea of a Vertical Village.

Luke: We're seriously committed to this idea of truly mixed-use development, which we believe is the future of high-density urban living. A single-use building is a little bit like single-use plastic – it doesn't fulfil the life cycle benefits embodied in creating that product. Taking the regular uses, like retail and office space, and stacking them vertically, gives a building or a precinct a 24-hour lifecycle. People can wake up in their apartments, turn on the TV, have a shower, then leave for work within the same building or go to a nearby building, while other people come into the building to use the office or retail spaces.

Aaron: Are there ways of offsetting those uses to allow for more affordable housing in the development? What kind of uses could go in there and allow for greater accessibility?

Luke: We are working hard to have a full range of price points. Mixed-use gives the financial model many other levers, more than just building and selling apartments. Different financial models, such as hotels, offices or retail, can sit on top of each other.

Aaron: The procurement and financing model becomes interesting for a mix-use development. It naturally starts to change the typical developer model for residential works.

Luke: It is also a lot more work. For commercial offices, the current trend is to have a side core to allow for flexible floor space. In one of our towers, for example, we have a hotel on top of some offices, and a side core is the worst arrangement for a hotel. So we're weighing up the pros and cons of each core arrangement to determine how these uses can work together. We're also working with a double-decker lift system that serves both the offices and the hotel. There are complexities to it, but that doesn't mean that it's not worth doing.

John: These kinds of planning complexities are familiar to architects. I'm curious about the financing – the average bank would probably find these models a little bit difficult to comprehend.

Luke: We're looking at a five to six-year build for the two towers I mentioned. Commercial tenants aren't looking that far ahead - they are generally three years ahead. So we'll be three years into building the project before a principal commercial tenant will sign a lease. We can't get financing for that commercial part of the project without the pre-lease. So we need to break the financing packages down within one structure to almost bite-sized financeable components.

John: Mixed-use development is a significant part of how a city increases density and how it is partitioned up. If you fold things into one space, you achieve a type of compression, which refers to the conversation about tightening cities. If you don't need to go anywhere other than your immediate building or precinct, 20 to 30% of a city's floor area can be removed or repurposed. Rather than a small apartment, you've got a smaller city.

Luke: Another development model is the joint venture. I know a lot of developers that want to work with this model in the future. In very simple terms, you own a block of land, and you want to sell your house. If you contribute the land component, the developer doesn't need a loan or pay interest to buy that land. The developer can invest what they would typically spend on land finance into building the project well and pricing it well.

John: Yes, cities are full of landholders who don't have the capital to do what you're describing.

Aaron: This point also leads to questions around sharing risk. There is a sense that consultants or local governments don't have any skin in the game.

John: Risk is at the core of a lot of these projects, both financial risk and for cities. A lot of anxiety around density is a lack of knowledge or familiarity with different models. Developers bear a lot of that risk: they are subject to the whims of public opinion, planning structures and political processes.

Luke: There are easier ways to make money. People in property development for the right reasons are doing it because they want to create great spaces.

Graham: It's not often you speak to a developer who thinks very passionately about the qualities of a city. Having said this, they're barely given a chance to talk about these ideas.

Aaron: We need to demonstrate that living in a very dense city can be great. And that living in a dense environment can be as good, if not better, than the great Australian dream in the suburbs. If we can develop ways of living densely that are particular and enjoyable, then that would limit the risk for future development.

23

Interview with Ruben Bergambagt, Dutch architect and founder of Beijing-based office Superimpose

Ruben: We started to look into the *super tight* concept, and found that it occurs here in Beijing in a distinct way. For example, it is common to have large civic squares in front of the train stations, however, these spaces are so often empty. There are eight-lane ring roads in the city. Tiananmen Square is one of the biggest squares in the world. Everything is spaced out and oversized. When I moved to Beijing, I tried to cycle from the Forbidden City to the Olympic Park. Reading the map, I thought it was probably half an hour. It took me three hours. The city's so big, and the city blocks are set up in such a way that it is not a city to walk. You always feel you are too far away from everything.

However, we can find tightness in Beijing. We believe it is happening in two ways. Firstly, because it is difficult to access different parts of the city due to infrastructure limitations, you almost feel pressed together. And on the other hand, there are the old *hutong* spaces in Beijing that might seem *tight* but feel spacious.

There are two types of Beijing. There is the old and the new Beijing. In the new Beijing, everything is spaced out, while in the old Beijing, the *hutongs* are compressed, and it is here where we can feel this sense of tightness. We started to develop an interest in these two opposites. We talked about non-physical *tightness* and physical *tightness* – the feeling of *tightness* and actual *tightness*.

John: At a certain point, you said there is a compression that happens as a result of that excess scale. The observation is that people are compressed into the margins of the city, and within the block, there is also congestion. Where you have your office in Sanlitun is an example of this vibrancy.

Ruben: Actually, this is an older neighbourhood. This space is quite comfortable because everything is close. There are a diversity of functions: from restaurants to schools to offices and bars.

Where we have our office can be compared to the *hutongs*. The streets and surrounding spaces are smaller, and people are doing different activities.

John: These areas seem to follow a more iterative approach where the layers regenerate over time, as opposed to other parts of the city that appear flat and one scale.

Ruben: There is a retail area named TaiKoo Li in Sanlitun which was developed by a Hong Kong developer. It is the most successful retail development in Beijing and perhaps in China. They managed to move away from the big shopping mall block superblock, which is everywhere in Beijing. It is a place where people can parade and take a walk. But it's the only pedestrian retail space which I know of in Beijing. You can see that there is a big need for people to go to places where they can avoid cars and walk small distances between shops and other functions. This is a good example of how it should be in the city.

Graham: Beijing's hardly the only city in the world to be over-scaled for pedestrians, but it does seem extreme. I'm curious about the first thing you said, that Beijing feels like it's designed for double the population or more people. Do you have some thoughts about the notion of backfilling the city? Can you imagine that scenario where Beijing becomes more inwardly dense, or will it simply sprawl like many other cities?

Ruben: It's going to sprawl, this is already happening. The government has currently put a cap of 25 million people in Beijing. They're moving the administrative part of Beijing outside the city to an area called Tongzhou, which is a one hour drive from the centre. They are not looking at densifying. In fact, they are trying to get people out of the city and make the city smaller. But it feels like the city is designed for double the number of people. It is built into the planning regulations – everything needs to be on a large scale. There is so much excess space around the buildings.

Graham: As you were talking, I was thinking of the analogy of buying a pair of pants that are twice the size so you can grow into them. It is funny to suggest that you would do that at the same time as depopulating a city, which is what is happening in Beijing.

This development model and the obsession with infrastructure that accompanies it is geared up to accommodate future population growth and flows. These spaces are modelled around maximum use here in China, and you don't understand the scale until you see them during Golden Week or the New Year. I'm wondering if there is an alternative model to planning, which allows a loose fit approach to city-making. One that also allows for massive growth or flows. This idea of potentially over-scaling everything for it to be backfilled is interesting in this context. But is this the only way? What we are talking about isn't a loose fit. Is it? It is something entirely other than that. It is a combination of things being over-scaled but also very tightly regulated.

John: If I can change course slightly, what is your view of the hutongs? They are often viewed and modelled in the west as good examples of fine-grain density. How are they perceived in Beijing?

Ruben: The *hutongs* are the most characteristic area of Beijing. As a westerner living in Beijing, I often went there because it reminded me a little bit of living in Europe. Those parts of the European city where you can walk, you can explore, and you're close to other people. Now, it is a tourist area. It has changed a lot. Many hutongs have been demolished. Previously, it was an area where there were a lot of bars. The fun part of Beijing used to be in the *hutongs*. A few years ago, they broke up all those little bars and shops. The government cracked down on illegal commercial spaces and changed them back into residences. The *hutongs* are still the most beautiful and most characteristic area in Beijing. But it just doesn't work for the city anymore, Beijing continues to modernise.

Graham: When we talk about density, the *hutongs* are not that dense compared to other types of cities. Even the more traditional areas of Shanghai, I have found, are more dense than the *hutongs*.

Ruben: Yeah, they feel dense in the street, however, they are not dense if you talk about the number of people living there.

John: Traditionally they were not only living places but also included workspaces, workshops and retail. This is also a form of *tightness*. They're adaptable as well. Plumbing and modern services are a bit tricky, but they can be divided effectively. Each *hutong* can be a residence for a large family and made into smaller units.

Ruben: Yes, a lot of people, all the workers, share rooms together.

Graham: I'm wondering whether there are lessons in developing new housing or urban models that are denser and have greater amenity. Is there something that could be drawn from these places and translated into a new model of architecture? It isn't necessarily a copy of the past but a proposition that draws on some of the performative qualities of those spaces.

Ruben: Firstly, I would think about the feeling of community in the *hutongs*, which is completely missing in these new cookie-cutter developments. It is impossible to leave your house without being noticed – people talk to each other, there is intimacy. Who cleans up the garbage? Who cleans the toilet? Everybody has a small job, and there is a community there for each other. Everybody does something to help. Kids are being watched by the neighbours, for instance. This feeling of community is how I grew up in the Netherlands. I have the feeling for the importance of having a neighbour who can mean something to you. It happens in the *hutongs*, and it is missing in all the new developments.

John: Are there any examples where that is not the case? Perhaps Steven Holl's *Linked Hybrid* building?

Ruben: The *Linked Hybrid* is a great design, but all bridges are currently closed off. The purpose of the linked hybrid is not being used according to its design intent. I think they're closed for management issues. This might be to do with fire egress, or maybe they don't want people lingering around.

Graham: That sounds like the same urban problem that is being faced in many different places. It is not limited to China. It is a global problem. A lot of the things that you've been talking about, like unity and connectivity, are at the mercy of these restrictions. Basically, if space is set aside for things that don't fall within a type of individual ownership model, it is under threat. Development models push away the difficulty of dealing with these kinds of things. It is too difficult to control.

Ruben: Yes, indeed. We did a design for a theatre in an existing building. We proposed a big staircase for people to wait for their friends before they go into the show. The clients liked it, but they couldn't understand how they would manage that space. What if an older person sat down there? What if the local community wanted to use it? All of these scenarios were considered problems, so they took it out of the project.

This might be a worldwide phenomenon, but there is this attitude amongst many developers and planning professionals that we should not give away our square metres, which we paid for, to the public. They don't care about public staircases where people can meet and have their lunch together. It is a pity.

John: If we go back to Taikoo Li in Sanlitun as an example, it was a successful retail area at a time when shopping centres were dying. This was happening in the outer parts of Beijing and throughout China. It is thriving because it offers an experience that is not focused on consumption.

Ruben: People are not always there to buy something. It is a place to be and to meet other people.

24

Spacious Tightness

Superimpose

As the name suggests *Spacious Tightness* explores the disconnect between physical form and sensation. Specifically, it explores the idea that physical space cannot be fully equated to a non-physical experience (such as the sense of spaciousness or *tightness*). A *loose* space can be made to feel *tight*, and a *tight* physical space could be designed to feel spacious.

Superimpose explore this idea in the city of Beijing, where their office is based. The vast arterial networks and public spaces of Beijing can often feel constricted and congested, despite their enormous scale.

They explore the potential for *tightening* Beijing's public spaces through a small-scale installation in public courtyard in Beijing's Chaoyang district. The installation works to form a room within a larger courtyard, creating a concentrated *tight* space that intensifies the experience of the existing elements within the courtyard. It serves as place of seclusion and quiet contemplation by day, while at night it can be activated as an event and performance space for the neighbourhood.

The project suggests that quality public space, focused around desirable forms of density and *tightness*, has the potential to convey a greater sense of joy than undifferentiated open space.

25

Singapore Projects

WOHA

The Singapore context is a particular test case for *tight* urbanism, being both a hot humid climate and centrally controlled and planned. The tendency for design in tropical climates is toward dispersal, paradoxically mirroring modernist planning principles (Oasia Hotel Downtown).

WOHA's body of work consistently looks for the intensity of the *tight* city with the *looseness* of tropical environment, under the constraint of contemporary development models in Singapore. Their projects explore approaches through which the envelope or organisation of a building is perforated or made porous, allowing vegetation or outside air to enter. (Pickering Hotel Singapore).

Covered open space, sheltered from sun and rain, is a critical form of social and public space. The porosity and provision of unprogrammed semi-public space allows for a loose fit, flexible use by residents and the public. (Kampung Admiralty Singapore)

26

A conversation with Hu Yan and Li Han, partners in Drawing Architecture Studio based in Beijing

Hu Yan: We would like to give everyone a little bit of background information about the Chinese urban village, which is the subject of this piece, *Diamond Village* included in the Super Tight project. The urban village is a concept or a housing model. The reason why we have urban villages is that according to the land property policy in China, as a citizen in the city you don't own any land. You cannot buy a piece of land and build your own house. But for residents in the rural countryside, each household can have a small piece of land for their own house. Usually households will just build a small house for their own use.

But some villages were really close to the cities, and as the city developed it grew around the village. As the city population increases, many people from the countryside want to come to the city for work but they cannot afford to live there. So they started to live in these villages, which are technically outside of the city. So, the villagers see the opportunity to build very high-density housing.

Li Han: Yes, to get more rent.

Hu Yan: However these villages were later included in the administration of the city. So they became urban villages. Shenzhen is a very unique city in China because it started 40 or 50 years ago. It was like a village, or at least a small town, because of the special economic policy it grew very fast. Now it is one of the megacities in China. Many young people came to Shenzhen over the years to make their living, and the villagers started to create these high rise buildings. One example is Nantou. It is a very big urban village in the downtown area. Very close to some new facilities, expensive apartments, and shopping malls. Those that live in Nantou feel that they live in the city – it is not disconnected. However, due to the density and the height of these buildings, many of the laneways feel very dark even in the daytime.

In 2017, the Shenzhen Biennale was held in this area; it was a very big event organised by the government. This event shows that to some extent the government was also keen to keep this place rather than removing it. I suppose that it is also because there are too many people living here and it is too expensive to change it to something else and relocate people. So they tend to keep those urban villages in Shenzhen.

Li Han: There is another urban village in Shenzhen called Yu Tian, which is the site for our *Diamond Village* drawing. In this area, we can see some modifications of the existing urban village by developers and local government. Typically, they will buy these high rise buildings from the farmers or maybe rent them for 20 years and renovate them to a better standard. They put in some public facilities such as bridges to connect the areas and provide accommodation for young people working in Shenzhen. When we went to this site, we felt that, although it's very tired, it feels pretty comfortable and very convenient because it is located in the centre of the city and close to the subway system. It has all these facilities you can use, high-quality office buildings and the shopping malls are all close. So you feel as though you're living in the city, although it's not a luxury area. In some ways, the urban village has become a fashionable lifestyle choice for young people.

And the Yu Tian village has two grids, a 45 degree angle grid and a 90 degree angle grid. When we saw this we remembered the *Diamond House* by John Hejduk. There are certain similarities in the plan.

Hu Yan: In producing this drawing, we opened up the laneway in the centre. We hoped to show the life on the street. To the side, we used a different projection to illustrate the density. We completed three drawings of this area to play with visibility.

Li Han: The laneway in the urban village is pretty narrow, but there are a lot of things happening in these spaces. If we drew the projection in the same direction, the laneway would be hidden by buildings. So in the middle, we projected the buildings in different directions.

John: You've managed to unfold the city, pulling back the buildings to get into the street. One of the things that we've been talking about in this exhibition is the porosity of density. How do you make decisions about what you show in these drawings?

Li Han: Firstly, it's about the building and which part is more interesting to us. Whichever facade we select will determine how we project the drawing. We also feel it's much more interesting to show the interior of Chinese cities. The exterior is typically not that good, especially in this area where you find boring walls and repetitive windows. But inside the building, there are so many things happening, and we dig into these areas to expose them.

Hu Yan: It's very important that we always try to take advantage of architectural drawing techniques. Like projection, sections, plans, everything that is unique about architectural drawing that you cannot achieve in photography, painting or perspective drawings to understand the city.

In the beginning, our drawings were single projections. Later, we formed these multiple projections with visual illusions. Through this technique, we have more possibilities to show the part that cannot be seen in one single picture. By manipulating these projections, it unfolds more content. So that is one way to make the drawing dense.

Vicky: When you talk about documenting the city, what kind of accuracy do you want to achieve?

Li Han: We try to keep everything close to reality – this is one of our main principles. Also, we think the real world is sometimes more interesting than our own imagination.

Hu Yan: Everything requires editing. All the details are from reality, but probably the final results are a little bit different. You can still see it is familiar. We want to achieve a balance of these two qualities.

John: How full is too full? When do you stop? Have you ever got to the point where a drawing is too full?

Li Han: At the beginning of the drawing, we will decide on the final exhibition scale. We want to always achieve an even density throughout the work.

Vicky: There is also something traditional about the way you approach these drawings. The drawing's density seems to be determined by the sheet of paper and which pen to use.

Li Han: We realised we are traditional when we started this practice. We like to see the drawings printed out to decide on the details to help communicate how to move forward.

Graham: Maybe we could talk a little bit about this idea that the mechanisms or the methods of the discipline are important to hold onto in talking about density. Usually, the conversation around density is dealt with by sociologists, economists, politicians, planners and newspaper pundits. Architects are usually the lackeys or the enablers of density rather than the authors of it. How important is it that we exercise disciplinary knowledge in this space?

Vicky: Firstly, it is important to document these spaces with measured architectural drawings. There is also an opportunity to recognise the agency within density. These drawings demonstrate that there are excellent spaces due to their *tightness*.

John: Scale also has a huge impact on what we think is possible in design. If we're designing cities at 1:10,000 scale, there seems to be a natural tendency to make everything too big. And *tightness* becomes the enemy.

Vicky: Cities often have a larger vision. At another scale, there are smaller innovations, anomalies and adjacencies where novel conditions emerge. There is something about these drawings that speak to how you generate freshness and surprise in a city. It operates at a certain scale.

Li Han: Right. I want to shift the conversation to talk directly about this issue of *tightness*. I think *tight* is a more amplified version of density. In Chinese, the word *tight* means interlocked to each other, not just dense. You can draw buildings, build them together, make them very tall, but the most interesting part is to organise these elements to ensure they are connected.

We can see examples of places in China where artists and the local people live together. It is not *tight* because there is no interaction. But in the Yu Tian example, there are a lot of interactions, and it's pretty *tight*. If the neighbours know each other, then that is *tight*. In the apartment building in Beijing, where we live, we don't know the neighbours. So even though we live closely together, it is dense but not *tight*.

Graham: It is fantastic to hear you articulate these differences and how the term operates in the Chinese language. We've talked a lot about the word *tight*, and you also used the term *interlocking*. Taishin Shiozaki talks about *overlapping* as a way of making things *tight*. For us, there's a level of precision in tightness which is not just about jamming things together, but in fact, making them fit and tuning them to that level of density.

John: Yes, and perhaps one of the great things about your drawings is that they exhibit a culture.

Hu Yan: We draw these places because once they are gone, they won't be recorded in architectural history. We are very interested in the daily lives and the conditions of the inhabitants. So, that is why we try to document and find our way to share what we have learnt about cities.

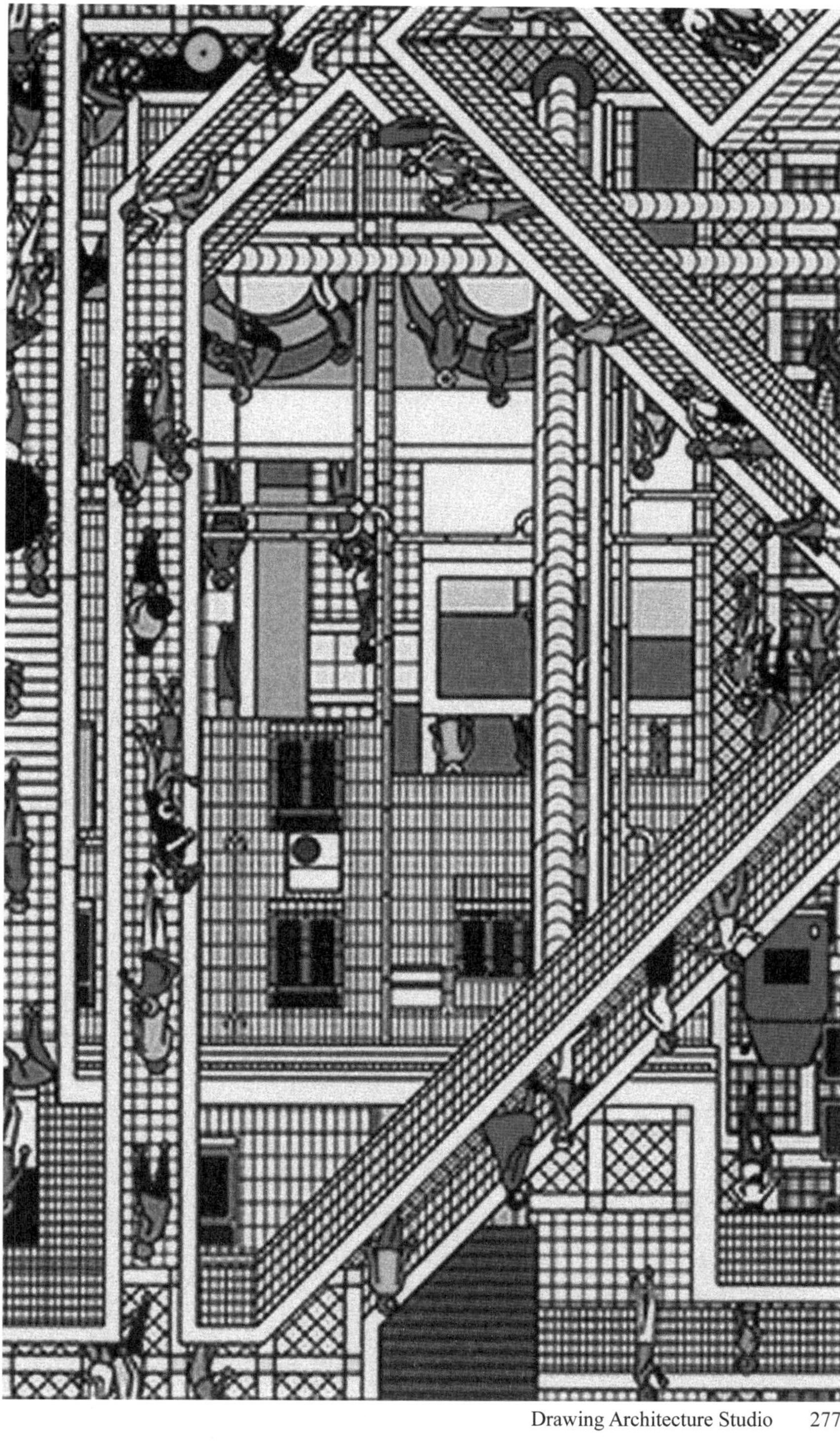

27

Diamond Village Series

Drawing Architecture Studio

Diamond Village is a series of drawings ilustrating a hypothetical urban scene that is based on observations of Yu Tian urban village in Shenzhen. The village was organised around a 45 degree grid, which is amplified and becomes the principal organising device of the drawing.

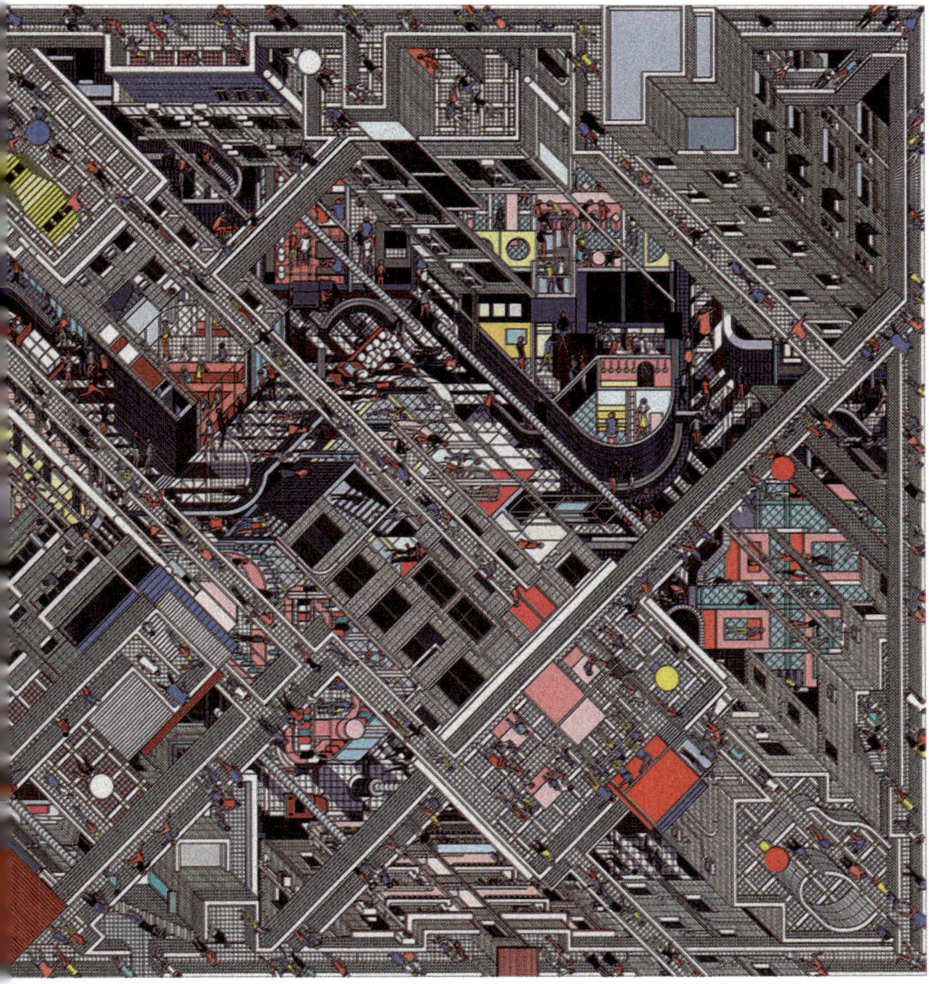

Drawing Architecture Studio use architectural drawing techniques such as projection and sectional cut-aways to reveal the occupation and interiority of urban environments. *Diamond Village* is drawn in three parts, each illustrating a different point in daily life, with shifting projection points highlighting changes in the way the city is occupied as it transitions from day to night.

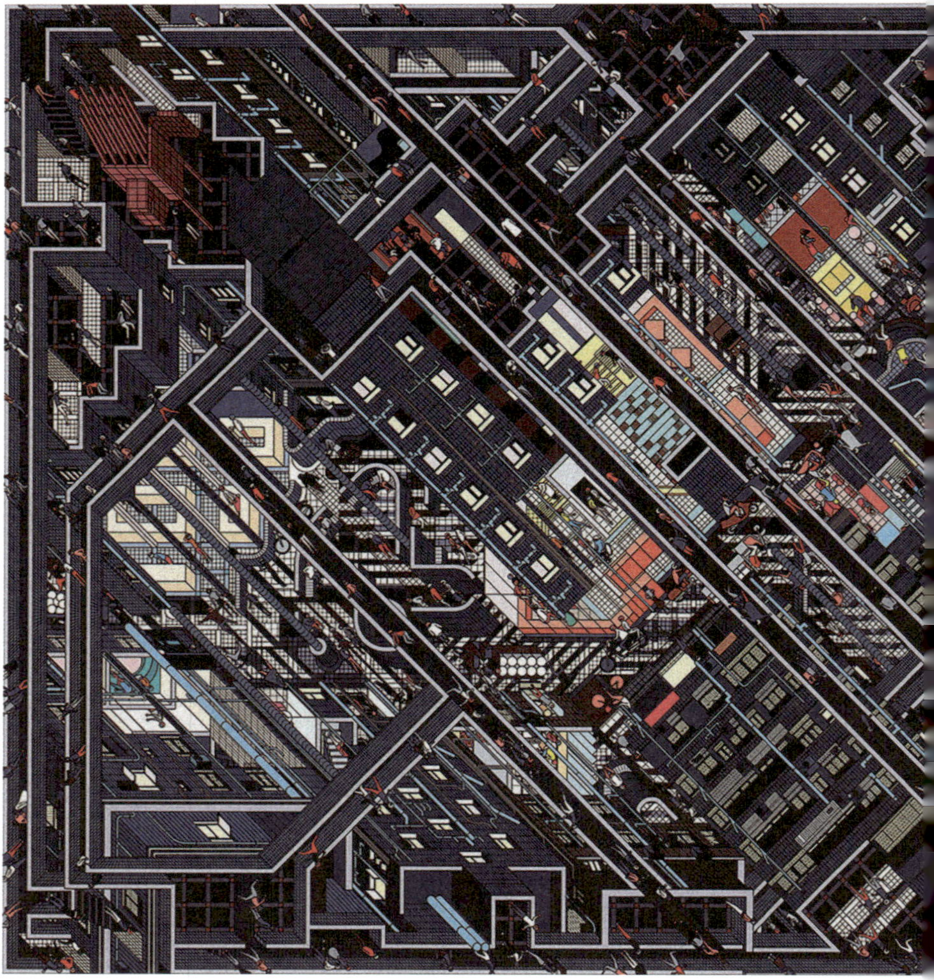

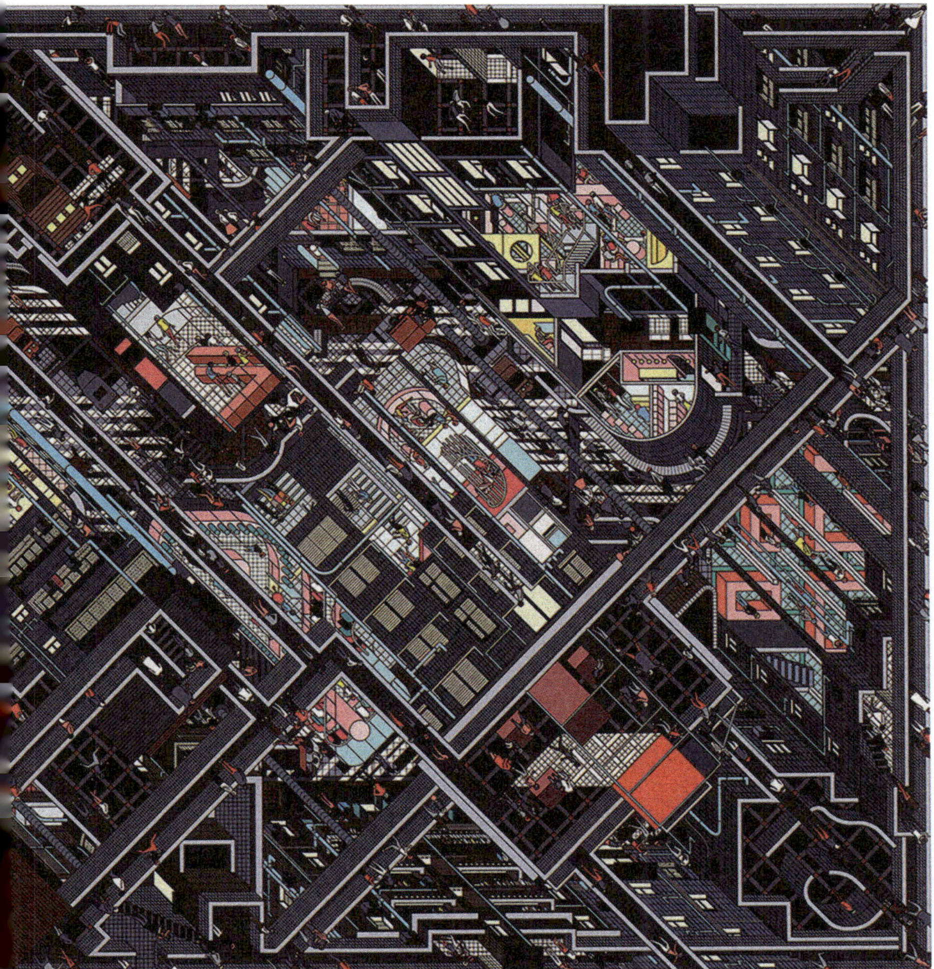

The work of Drawing Architecture Studio provides an example of how design and creative practices can draw on the lived reality of dense urban environments as a fountainhead of emergent urbanities.

28

A conversation with Maria-Luisa Nardella and Edward Service from the local government Moreland City Council on the Brunswick Design District regenerative project. We were also joined by Helen Duong.

Maria-Luisa: The Brunswick Design District came about through conversations with RMIT University and Creative Victoria. We were interested to learn what we could do as a group to enhance the activities that are already occurring in Brunswick. Through these conversations, we identified many opportunities that we could co-create, identify and recharge under-utilised spaces and find ways to build the capacity for design and creative industries within the precinct.

Edward: My role in the council is to support creative arts spaces. We see the creative industries, manufacturing, and arts as inextricably linked and connected to these types of areas.

Graham: We're conscious that gentrification goes with that process – as we watch the rise in property prices in places like Moreland. Yet generally, density is associated with poor quality, high-rise housing.

Maria-Luisa: That is the importance of good design in the housing market, of architects leading in design, taking into consideration long-term sustainability, social spaces, and the capacity to build a sense of community and strong neighbourhood. In local government, we have limited power to control gentrification. The influence of design exemplars in the city is important – to demonstrate what we would like to see more of and help accelerate our projects. The big concern for developers is often profitability, and when that is the priority, it's hard to get a nuanced design within particular residential builds. This doesn't stop us from thinking about what we can work on, like open space, for instance, and how we can use our influence to bring more ideas to how designs are delivered.

Edward: Once we see examples that show the value of a building's proximity to other activities, it becomes more convincing. The problem is relying on the private market to deliver all our infrastructure.

Graham: It is interesting that the discussion goes immediately to questions of control versus the market. The importance of demonstration projects is interesting too. A lot of demonstration projects from other cities wouldn't conceivably be possible in any planning scheme in Australia.

Maria-Luisa: It is about having the imagination to show how you use spaces flexibly. We know that we have lots of spaces in our city that wouldn't sit well with regulatory or policy principles, but we recognise that we need to liberate them. We need to put levers in place that encourage it to happen.

Helen: In Brunswick, people park where they want; people put their bikes where they want, and they put their rubbish where they want. These systems perhaps make the public realm look unsafe and aren't aesthetically pleasing. But these slippages and examples of density and overlap are a quality people in Brunswick want to retain.

Edward: Sometimes the best places to live are not the most efficient or meet all the policy criteria. For example, these former industrial areas should be terrible places to live, but people love being there. This idea of an imperfect urban realm and why that is so attractive creates a massive dilemma for government planning.

Maria-Luisa: Our population is invested in our city. There is a sense of ownership in a changing and diverse population. There is a lot of activity on the street, which makes this apparent. We're never going to have a perfect footprint, Brunswick will always be a place of transition and hyperactivity.

Helen: The idea of transition is interesting and more apparent in Brunswick than in some other places. There is potential for you to do that thing you're not sure you've got permission to do. You do it and then see if it works.

Graham: When a city is finished, it is incredibly boring. A less than ideal urban apartment is a trade-off to be in that city. How much can you give up in a dwelling to live in a particular part of the city?

Maria-Luisa: The evidence for this comes through engagement and consultation. Councils want to make significant contributionsto the public realm, especially in having more accessible open space. These include getting more cars off the street, having more capacity for public transport, walking, and cycling. Waste and the circular economy is becoming more pronounced in our city as well, so we are encouraging our population to be responsible for what they create. Our project is about understanding what spaces there are and what might the uses be in the future. Understanding that space is valuable, so how can we maximise it for now and for future uses.

Graham: There is a strong negative association with urban density; it is seen as something we need to limit. If we set a minimum density to achieve a real city, then it would change the conversation.

Edward: There are also many examples of bad apartments, visually unattractive apartments. We need more good examples.

Helen: There are tall buildings everywhere that are not very dense, but collectively they create a sense of density. There are three storey buildings that are dense but don't feel dense. So other environmental factors influence how you perceive your surroundings; it's useful to consider the spatial qualities of urban density - can you see enough of the sky or the opening at the end of the block or someone's face on a balcony? These are qualities of a comfortably dense city.

Graham: There is a relationship between perceived density and how much a population moves around. The more mixed a place is and the fewer people commuting creates a reduced perception of density.

Edward: Yes, and the ground floor interface is critical. In Melbourne, there are so many car park entrances that disrupt how these spaces look and feel.

KALDI COFFEE FARM
KALDI COFFEE FARM
KALD

29

A conversation curated by Jana Perkovic from Assemble Papers with Andy Fergus (City of Melbourne), Katherine Sundermann (MGS architects), Alexis Kalagas (urban strategist from the Urban Think Tank), Ihnji Jon (Connected Cities Lab Melbourne University), Ishita Chatterjee (Informal Research Hub at Melbourne University), Piers Morgan (Fieldworks), Mark Jacques (Openwork, RMIT Architecture + Urban Design)

Graham: What do you understand the term *super tight* to mean? Through this project, we've been advocating for the possibilities of hyper-density, with no necessary upper limit for any urban context.

Jana: *Assemble Papers'* tagline is the culture of *Living Closer Together*. It's a way to think about density and apartment living beyond architectural typology. Using fewer resources, less land and urban space requires sharing. It requires considering what you need to own and what you can borrow, and what kind of spaces can be shared. It means a different type of culture.

Katherine: Once you've had that lived experience, living in a detached house seems less appealing. Some things are much better in an apartment.

Mark: But I can't think of a culture that is more opposed to sharing infrastructure and opportunistic occupation than ours here in Australia. We have an ingrained disposition to mark out territory and defend it. If the purpose of *Assemble Papers* is to begin to unpack and challenge that culture, what other tools might we have as practitioners, policymakers? Unless we tackle those tendencies head-on, nothing changes.

Alexis: I'm interested in these questions around our culture and how it relates to the built environment. In the City of Melbourne, 56% of the residents are born abroad, and where these residents grew up shapes their propensity to live in proximity to others. For instance, I grew up in a forest with plenty of land outside every dwelling. But our generation now finds owning a detached house and commuting to the city almost impossible. This is a consequence of many factors, many of them economic.

Jana: Coming here for the first time in 2004, everyone was saying, 'We are a suburban nation, we need a ton of space.' My first memories of Melbourne were the small bars. I could not understand why people wanted to be in such tight spaces and the idea that Australians needed lots of space.

Ishita: Coming back to your initial question, I think about *tightness* at a completely different scale. I understand living and culture beyond the walls of the house. In other words, many functions can't be accommodated by the home. *Tightness* is felt not only in rooms and buildings but also in the streets and neighbourhoods. There are hierarchies and layers to these spaces. *Tightness* also expands and contracts based on activities and times. In the houses of informal settlements I've visited, there is often a lane on both sides of the dwelling; a back lane and front lane. As a visitor, it's impermeable because I could not cross inside the house; whereas for that community living there, they cross through the houses internally. I realised that in the morning they don't close the doors; the curtains are drawn but you could just walk in; at certain other times of the day, the doors remain closed. As an outsider to this neighbourhood, there were things I didn't understand about this form of *tight* living.

Alexis: Compare that network of spaces that a child can colonise to a city like Tokyo, where you might live incredibly close to one another, but your ability to move between buildings is different. So it is both the dwelling and how we inhabit these neighbourhood spaces during the day.

Ihnji: The cultural perception of beauty in dense settlements interests me. Coming from Seoul, I was used to middle-class people living *tightly*. But for friends in Paris, there are negative connotations attached to high-rise living: it is equated with certain socioeconomic conditions. I was exploring suburbs outside Paris, and other students were shocked. They would say, 'You can't go in there. It's dangerous.' For me, it was normal and unproblematic. The idea that dense living can be considered beautiful is changing. Japanese architects and designers are proving that dense living doesn't mean a lack of creativity or public housing.

Jana: There is debate about whether living closer together makes life more sustainable, more resilient and whether it makes it easier for us to respond to the increasing climate emergency.

Mark: There is a persistent theme that high density works against generosity and beauty and is associated with poverty. It will require a massive cultural shift to remove these associations. It's also a question of how development is procured. In a competitive development model where everyone develops their patch, there is no incentive to share infrastructure. That is a cultural problem we need to bust. So, that cultural deprogramming isn't just a demographic question. It is both a challenge to the existing development model and the design process.

Jana: Being a designer means providing what people need. German law stipulates a square metre of children's playground per city inhabitant, regardless of age. It details what equipment children of different ages need. These documents ask, what do children need that goes beyond a backyard? What are the affordances of a house that need to be translated to an apartment building?

Piers: Here in Melbourne, it is easy to accommodate smaller apartments in developments. It's not difficult for an architect to design a 20 or 30 square metre apartment. The regulations, finance and market demands make it difficult. For instance, you can't get a loan for an apartment under 50 square metres, which means that developers struggle to sell them.

Andy: This leads to the form follows finance conversation. Architects act on client requirements; each development is affected by a range of external factors. A problem for finance is how we value space outside the purchased title. Financial instruments dictate minimums. The fifty square metre rule, for example, is imposed by banks because of resale value. In co-living or build to rent models, financial barriers to building smaller apartments are falling away. What is interesting is the difference between the ability to design a great small space and your license to do that within a fixed cost.

When you start building in flexible joinery, the cost of a small apartment becomes commensurate with a larger apartment. How do we regulate performance irrespective of the size?

Alexis: There are people working within the planning authorities who maintain the frameworks and minimum standards within which markets can operate. Co-living is a niche part of the market. It is never intended for a family or even for a couple. It is pitched at young, transitory professionals with good disposable incomes in big cities. These are people who don't have existing social networks and want to live in places to meet others. In Zurich, shared amenity is part of the co-operative housing market. So you can offer much lower rent and have better quality living spaces if you change the financial model. The culture of living in a cooperative way has formed as a consequence of economic forces. That culture takes time to emerge. Back in Australia, there are places in Sydney where people have been living in apartments for 60 years – they're not pining for the suburban block.

Andy: It is important to make clear comparisons when we use cities like Zurich or Copenhagen as examples. There are eight storey apartment buildings in Zurich for instance, with a plot ratio of 1.5, which is about a 20th of some recent Melbourne developments. By contrast, Melbourne has a two speed housing model: sprawl and hyper density. There is a need for other types that sit between those two models which industry can roll out.

Graham: I want to bring the conversation back to spaces in a city that encourage informal use, the spaces outside the home where we might have to share and live in proximity to others.

Ishita: I don't associate informal settlements with words like *tight* or compact. For me, it's about shared living. Informal settlements make things function well with less, in that sense, they are carefully designed.

Graham: And health problems continue to be conflated with density rather than being seen as the result of poverty.

Katherine: When informal settlements are eradicated, the replacement apartment block sometimes has much more significant problems. I don't advocate for a *tabula rasa* approach. I am more interested in upgrading without displacement and designing with the communities to maintain their strength. In Melbourne, market actors operate in an environment with no government subsidy, policy or strategy. Melbourne is moving from a suburban detached house model to a high rise model and skipping over planned, medium density environments.

Jana: What we can learn from informal settlements is the adaptability and flexibility it provides to residents. In New Orleans, after Katrina, a lot of public housing was torn down. This meant five or six storey buildings rather than twenty storey blocks. As a result of these developments, there emerged further tensions and racial disadvantages within the existing communities. They were evicting the people who couldn't afford to live in the new places.

Alexis: When we renew our social housing stock, we often tender large sites with multiple buildings. It is convenient to make such a large investment. What is missing are local investment models that build with a community. For example, the renewal precinct *Buiksloterham* in Amsterdam had a large-scale, top-down master plan. Luckily the GFC killed the project. The effect was that they tried a completely different model of urban development. They tendered sites for ten years, and architects, business partners, ecologists, whoever would take up these sites and experiment with what could be done. The government there used tools other than large scale centralised investment. They looked at how they could set up offices to test and review proposals at a finer scale. They iterated built projects up into the master plan from the bottom up. And they released sites for individual homes to benefit from collective action. Perhaps some of the most important urban renewals are those that reject large scale, convenient investment.

Ishita: Informal settlements are instructive in relation to all these questions. They can teach designers to give up a little bit of their control.

SPPL
पंचशील
SPPL
PANCHSHEEL
1

30

CASACO Project

tomito architecture

The *CASACO project* was the alteration and renovation of an existing house in the suburbs of Tokyo. The house was adapted to become a shared community building for a neighbourhood. The project demonstrates how design can play a role in adapting the urban environment for tight knit communities. To prepare for the project, tomito architecture undertook an extended briefing process with the local community. The outcome of this was a 'Local Ecology' map that documented the web of interlinked people and local groups, the history of the neighbourhood and mapped how the renovated building could serve the community.

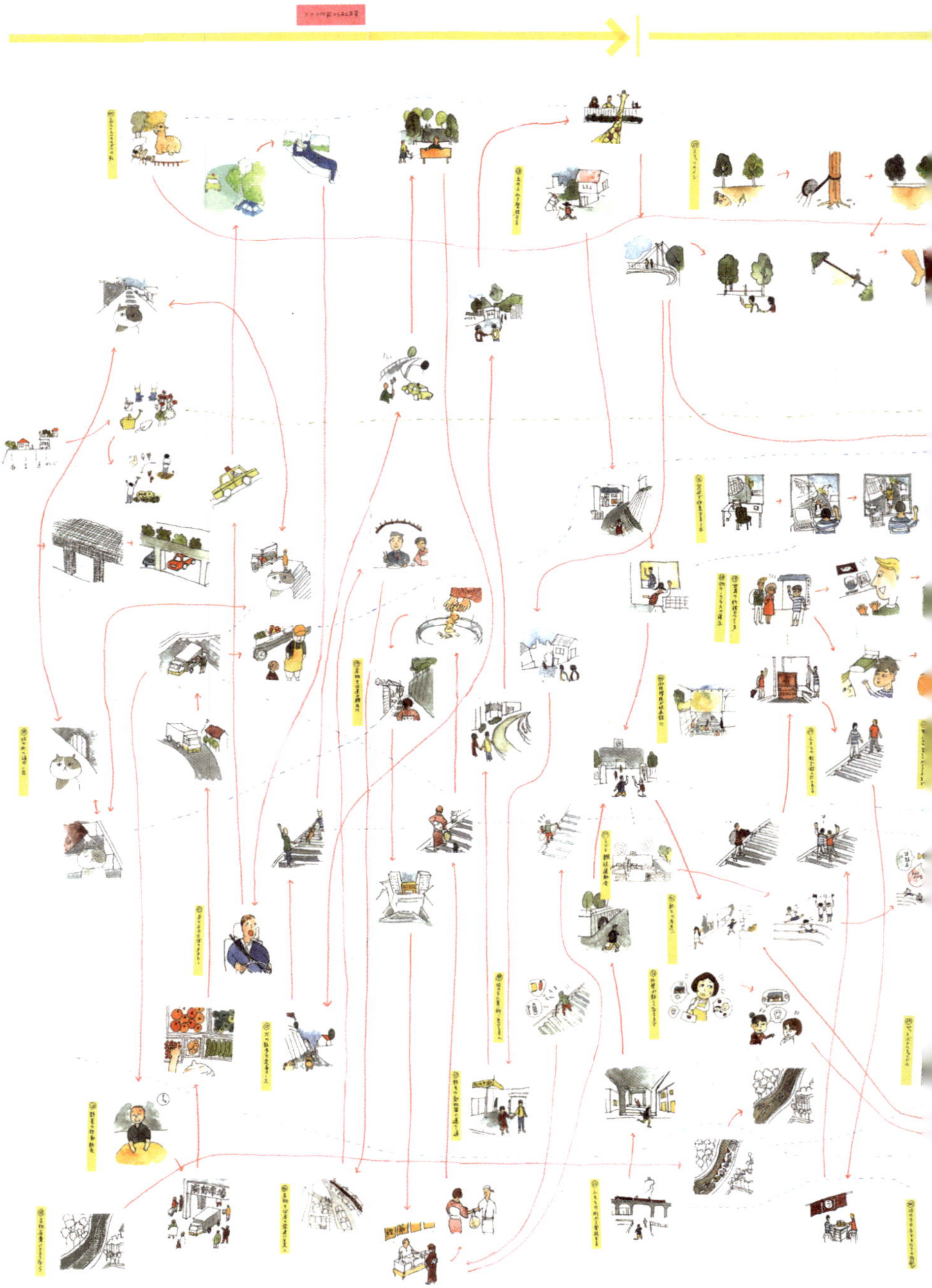

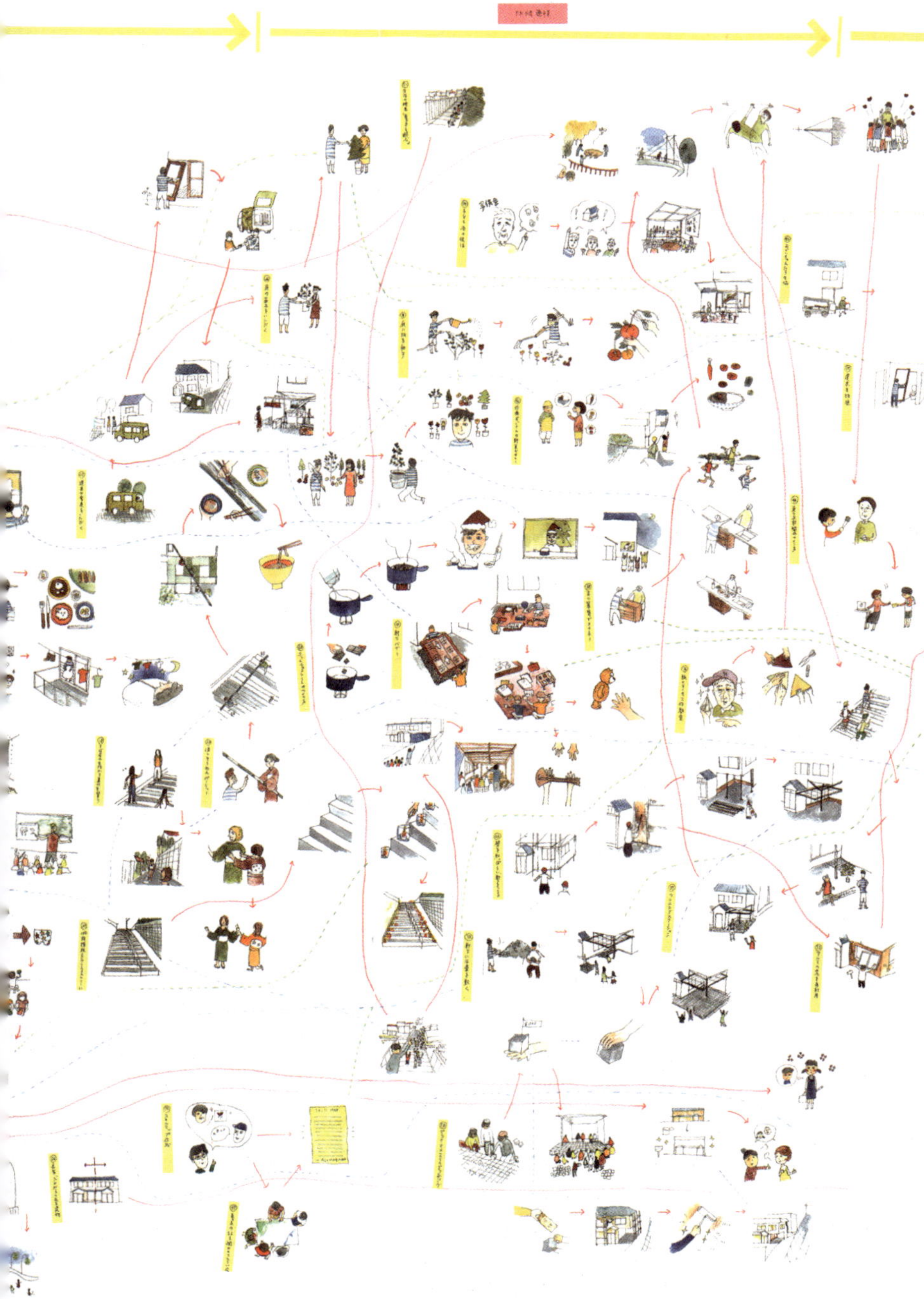

31

Tight and Tolerant Cultures

It is by coincidence that our use of the term *super tight* and our efforts to imagine the *tight* city crosses into Michele Gelfand's studies describing *loose* and *tight* cultures.[1] One uses the term *tightness* from the perspective of population psychology and social behaviours; the other through the lens of urban design and the city's physical form. However, the intersection of these ideas is crucial. Our attempts to articulate the *super tight* as an adaptation to urban density necessarily involves a series of behaviours that make living in a dense environment workable. We can describe *tightness* as a dense physical environment coupled with social patterns which reinforce its density. To understand the relationship between *tight* cultures and *tight* cities, it might be useful to reconceptualise density. Can a dense city be the host of a *loose* culture? Does a *tight* society necessarily adapt better to a denser environment? These questions are at the core of the problem of urban density. A *tight* culture is more adherent to social rules, and urban density is so often framed as coming at the expense of freedom. These terms are general and varied; the relationships are speculative, yet these speculations underpin design and policy. A presumption that urban density and stricter observance of rules converge in the term *tightness* needs to be scrutinised.

Gelfand's body of work on *tight* and *loose* cultures examines nations and communities and develops a comparative spectrum of *tightness* defined in terms of tolerance to deviation. A *loose* culture is open to diversity, values freedom and is permissive of a wide range of behaviours. At the same time, such societies tend to be less disciplined and orderly and averse to uniformity. The observations from these studies show that *loose* cultures have more addicts, more obesity, and their clocks are less synchronised. Even time is *looser*. Of course, *tight* cultures have more punctuality and are more inclined to follow a set of rules in an orderly way. They are less tolerant to foreigners, to unruly behaviours, and to change generally.

Robert Bruegmann's 2005 text, Sprawl: A Compact History, makes the case in favour of sprawled cities, or more specifically, it makes the case against the orthodoxies of controlling urban sprawl. The book takes on a debate against the 'coalition of architects, planners, academics, government officials and others across the affluent world (that) believes that sprawl is economically inefficient, socially inequitable, environmentally damaging, and ugly.'[2] Bruegmann constructs an image of sprawling cities as the enemy of those who would control development and the compact city growing begrudgingly out of necessity or from bureaucratic coercion. Therefore the sprawling city is a consequence of liberation from those constraints.

‘Historically the majority of cities took the shape they did not because anyone thought that this was ideal but because of the necessities of defence, accessibility and energy. Now that new technologies have loosened the noose, there is no reason why cities couldn’t look very different from the way they did in the 19th century.’[3]

The language is emotive. The dense city is a deadly oppressor – the city’s hangman. A sprawling city is historically and economically natural; it precedes the car and modernity, and sprawl is both the organic outcome of the free market and the aspiration of those who play and succeed in that market. By contrast, the modern compact city for Bruegmann is achieved only through authoritarian regulation, to which Soviet-era Moscow is a prime twentieth-century example. The argument outlined in *Sprawl* activates latent psychology in the modern planned city: density comes through suppression of freedoms and imposition of conforming regulations. Culturally, the tacit narrative of *Sprawl* suggests that urban density is too *tight* for the *loose*, freedom-loving modern citizens of the West and those who aspire to it.

Gelfand’s body of work speculates on some of the social factors which might influence a *tight* culture. One of the key influences for a culture to *tighten* is an external threat. This observation is understood in the broadest sense, irrespective of whether a threat is perceived or real. It is a generally observed principle that culture, or community, becomes *tighter* when under threat. For instance, a group becomes more observant of rules or norms and less tolerant of divergence from those norms when they are subject to external forces. Such tendencies are practical in a crisis: forming responsiveness and solidarity in wartime or a willingness to accept and follow restrictions on behaviours during a pandemic. *Tighter* societies are better geared to collectively mobilise. As a consequence of this, such principles might be exploited toward authoritarian ends. The construction of an external threat is useful for *tightening* a culture. It can help assert authoritarian rules and suppress or remove behaviours that do not follow a tightly defined pattern. A commonly observed example of a threat is poverty. The threat of poverty among those most vulnerable is a force that *tightens* culture, just as affluence can loosen the adherence to norms as the threat to economic stability recedes. Within a given group or society, the working classes tend to follow more strictly defined social values and be wary of values that sit outside those defined norms.

It is not surprising that Bruegmann might construct the twentieth-century struggle to control urban density as a battle of affluence won through market freedoms and rewarded with a sprawling city.

This struggle is opposed to the spectre of the Soviet city, with its totalitarian imposed poverty, matched by its gulag of high-rise apartments, formed through a consolidating master plan. These simplifications may seem melodramatic however the discussion of extreme density in western cities is often coloured with a touch of panic. In the *Sprawl* narrative, the low-density city is a natural expression of a successful property market and social freedoms. It is an analogue, by implication, of a *loose* culture.

Gelfand's work sets up a cultural binary. It does not advocate for the *loose* or the *tight:* it uses this binary as a comparative tool between cultures. It establishes a spectrum for understanding the cross-cultural extremes, and most importantly, for understanding the limitations or dangers of its extremes. While cultures vary, it is the middle ground of each which is desirable. The Goldilocks principle – not too hot, not too cold – as Gelfrand describes it, is an expression of a balanced sweet spot. Too much *tightness* suppresses innovation; too much *looseness* descends into a disorderly mess. The term *super tight*, as we use it, is open to the extreme. It responds to the urban planning notion that physical density should be tempered and limited. *Super tight* does not infer a maximum density but allows the possibility of more – beyond what current norms might suggest. This idea collides with the binary of an overcrowded city being both oppressively conformist and chaotically uncontrolled; that is both too loose and too *tight*. Culturally at least, this seems like a threatening situation.

So is density a threat? If a *tight* culture forms as a response to an external threat, is urban density a threat in itself? Gelfand has casually claimed that high density in cities is an example of a physical threat in the same way that invasion or persistent military attack might be threatening. External threats, like invasions or pandemics, need a coordinated and cooperative response best delivered by a *tightly* organised society. So density is framed as a psychological invasion by our too-close neighbours. Gelfand has suggested that urban density might trigger a need to *tighten* culturally, therefore, reducing our tolerance for difference. If cultural tightness is a reaction to threatening density, closeness and consolidation may be a response to threat. The pre-modern urban impulse was to gather tightly for safety, to squeeze behind the city walls for mutual protection. The physically *tight* city is both a threat and a response to a threat, and an observed response is to *tighten* culturally. Regardless of the varied circumstances, the discussion exposes the modern preoccupation with closeness as a form of threat, resulting in a loss of freedom. The social response to a dense urban environment is to *tighten* culturally, to forego the freedoms that come from tolerance and difference.

Archie Pizzini
Rasquachismo Series
Ho Chi Minh City

In the *super tight* city, where the agenda is to *tighten* the physical footprint, this relationship would need to be broken. It couples a tight urban structure with a loose tolerance and freedom, which facilitates the adaptations to density. Uncoupling physical tightness from threat might produce a tighter footprint; as well as social freedom with closeness.

Consider two cities that have become a focus of the Super Tight studies: Tokyo and Ho Chi Minh. How does the physical footprint interact with Gelfand's concepts of *tight* and *loose*? Both cities have been the locations of astounding external threats in the last century; chaos and destruction in the living memories of those in the city. Both have undergone very rapid economic expansion after wars. For Gelfand's studies, Japan is a benchmark for a very *tight* culture: orderly and homogenous in behaviours and norms. High levels of trust and safety exist within the very clean urban realm of Tokyo. Ho Chi Minh City, to the outsider, is observed as a wild and chaotic jungle by comparison. Both cities are known for their relatively low-rise but consistent density that extends over a large urban area. Both are also known for small or dense urban public spaces. Vietnam's urban environment and atmosphere is the antithesis of cities like Tokyo. The *tight* cultural orderliness is almost absent in the traffic flows, in the regulation of buildings, and in the occupation of street spaces. By Gelfand's criteria, Ho Chi Minh City's urban culture is a remarkably *loose* one. Given the centralised governmental control of Vietnam, it is even more remarkable. To the outside observer of Tokyo's public urban life, citizens have adapted to super-dense urban occupation through passive behaviours geared toward closeness. It is seen as a form of politeness suited to tolerating extreme proximity. It compresses the psychological bubble of personal space and ensures that on the surface, at least, it does not pierce the adjacent one. Medical masks were common on streets and trains long before COVID-19, one example of a relative muteness geared toward squeezing together.

Tourists can witness the remarkable quietness of a Tokyo train with its inhabitants quietly texting, sometimes whispering, and they can also witness the stoic, silent persistence of the urban crowd in a crushed queue. Ho Chi Minh City's lively street culture, for which this south-east Asian city is well known, comes from extreme occupation of the street. The boulevards teeming with motorbikes and cars and noise; the local laneways of the older quarters are quieter; the motorbikes persist slowly, and neighbourhood chatter is audible. Common to each space is the extreme occupation of the street: selling, buying and relaxing. The culture that works with this and supports it has a strong tolerance for noise and disturbance and relative indifference to privacy. The division between the space of a shop or café and the home is extremely blurry. The house, just like the streets, is layered with clear private barriers barely existent.

Video stills from
Beka and Lemoine film,
Moriyama-san, 2017

Is this culture one of extreme *looseness* as described by Gelfand? It seems paradoxical that a different form of social *tightness* occurs in these conditions – solidarity and intimacy that has adapted to the closeness of urban life.

Perhaps the *loose* and *tight* binary dissolves in the instance of some cities; perhaps this is simply a parallel discussion with unrelated definitions of loose and *tight*. It is also possible that there is little relationship between cultural *tightness* and the physical form of the city in which it is housed. Urban density, especially as it is described in places like Tokyo and Ho Chi Minh City, may have little correlation with cultural *tightness* or *looseness*. Designed projects may also form the exceptions to such rules. Japanese architectural culture may reflect and possibly benefit from a typically *tight* culture, but it may also give expression to the exception. It could at times be described as a project of *loosening* a culture.

The documentary film *Moriyama-san* (2017) by Beka and Lemoine depicts the celebrated Moriyama house in Tokyo designed by Ryue Nishizawa. It does this with focus on its owner and the social group he gathers in this setting. Through the film, we experience the intimacy and casual interaction framed by the tautly composed set of ten white architectural boxes. They have a careful but loose arrangement – the spaces between these boxes and the shared garden they create are set at ambiguous distances. The composition is like a diagram of the *loose*, *tight* binary: tightly designed cubes of space set to form loosely defined interactions. The small community formed by these houses is similar: taking the eccentricities of its spaces and of its owner as a counterpoint to the rules of their own orderly culture. The Fuji kindergarten in suburban Tokyo which famously commissioned Tezuka Architects to build the roof of its building for its children to wildly run on, created a comparable condition. It sensed the capacity for their architectural spaces and their piece of the city to foster future rule breakers.[4]

So what is most critical is for us to decouple the *super tight* city from a requirement for a socially *tight* culture. That is, to decouple urban density from the notion that it reflects conformity and intolerance to difference. A super-dense city with an urban culture that is *loose* enough to tolerate flux and variation would be an ideal combination of physical closeness coupled with cultural tolerance. It is possible even that the intense interactions of close contact might foster the loose behaviours which tolerate diversity. More likely and more possible is an oscillating co-existence of the *loose* and the *tight*, a set of adaptations allowing toleration of close cohabitation, and managed just *tightly* enough to make it collectively possible. Rather than simply striking a middle ground between the two, it finds the value of both ends of the *loose* and *tight* spectrum.

32

A conversation with Taishin Shiozaki from Shiozaki Laboratory, Tokyo, Marika Neustupny from NMBW and Desirée Grunewald, Illustrator based in Spain and Vietnam

Taishin: I would like to introduce an idea of overlapping and how it relates to *super tight* cities. This is a concept we have been discussing in my laboratory for the past three or four years and is explored further in our contribution to this exhibition. I think a *super tight* condition is a type of overlapping condition. How functions might overlap in space is fundamental to this concept of *super tight*. And *tightness* is, of course, related to density.

Density emerges from capitalism. It has been associated with a kind of chaos in the city, but we think there is a more important aspect to what we call the *super tight*. *Tightness* creates a sense of familiarity in a local community. We wanted to show examples of *tightness* because it is exactly the kind of overlapping condition that is common in our daily life. I want to start with my favourite painting; a painting by Pieter Bruegel named *Netherlands Proverbs* from the sixteenth century. There are so many activities and maybe accidents and behaviours occurring in this painting. Every action is happening at once. This kind of overlapping of many functions is the city; it is our urban situation.

The modernists in the twentieth century divided our daily lives into clear functions: working, living, recreation and resting. We need to return to the overlapping life. Overlapping has richness and diversity. Overlapping may have something to do with memory. Overlapping events, places, friends and activities become memories. We can say that overlapping is naming; it gives a sense of character to the things or the spaces. So in this exhibition, we tried to show two types of *tightness*. In zone one, we have 'the density of things'. It shows hyperdense situations based on the efficiencies we associate with capitalism. One example we explored was the capsule hotel: the capsule tower for humans, and next to that is a capsule for shops, a capsule for selling things, a capsule for storage, a capsule for comic reading and a capsule for parking a car.

In zone two, we show 'human activity and noise'. These drawings are *tight* situations where people must find appropriate forms of behaviour to survive in these conditions. For example, one guy must find a way to read a newspaper in the Japanese rush hour train – this is what we call a 'quattro-bended newspaper'. We can also see someone spying into a private space for entertainment on the train. There are so many tactics to survive in tight, dense situations.

Zone three is also a high-density example, but in this area, the people are having fun, laughing and talking to make a *tight* community. We call this 'tight familiarity'. This is in the Yokocho area. These kinds of tiny bars exist around Tokyo in very narrow streets. In these spaces, there are no borders. It just opens onto the very narrow street – which could be reminiscent of some of the laneways behind terrace houses in Australia. Unlike the terrace house, however, this is the front road for the houses in this area, so this is where everybody sees each other and interacts.

In another example, we show a seasonal festival. It is an emergent space, and it also reveals a *tight* familiarity. Overlapping is where a part of the city sometimes changes and becomes very full or dense and *tight*. All cities have these kinds of festivals; they are temporal phenomena. We describe these events and the effect they have on the city as 'critical double functionalism'. It is different from CIAM's definition of the functional city. We could also describe this as a 'two-way city' or a 'reversible city'. The example we have used is an *O-Hanami* cherry blossom viewing which occurs in parks and occasionally next to tombs. So adjacent to our ancestors, we have a party every year.

In the last part of our exhibition, zone six, we show the overlapping city, both public and private space. Many young people in Japan have an online life through virtual networks, so they're living in several worlds at once. They can change their identity in each account. In this section, we explore location-based games. *Pokemon GO* is a common game. So there are now so many worlds connected to this location.

The characters in this scene occupy the real world but also stand in their gadget world. The background is the actual world, and this is based on Tokyo. Using urban space for sports is another kind of overlapping.

This idea can be applied to architecture. In the laboratory, we are exploring how an overlapping city might become an analogy for a single room in a dwelling. In one room, we can share many kinds of behaviours or many activities at the same time. This idea is something I have tried to achieve in my work. For every design, we always try to make a one-room house.

Desirée: I am also studying this idea of overlapping in cities. I'm focussing on the alleys in Saigon which are called *hẻms* in Vietnamese. There are many overlapping layers and activities in these alleys. In one sense, it is the overlapping of noise and sound caused by all of the different activities. And it is also the overlapping and layering of textures, materials and different rhythms that constantly happen at the same time in the street. You can see the overlapping in the materials, how the houses touch each other and how the objects contain traces of the activities that happen in the street.

Taishin: I have never been to Saigon. When we discussed this exhibition space, it was suggested that we divide the gallery into narrower spaces. If we make it narrower, then it becomes *tighter*. People become closer, and as a consequence, activities become closer. Maybe this is an important phenomenon to think about for the *super tight* concept.

John: Yes, one quality of these kinds of narrow spaces, such as the *hẻms* or laneways, is to limit an individual's view of the city – you can't see everything at once. One fascinating thing about *tightness* as a spatial concept is that you never get an overview of anything. We usually talk about cities from a top-down view, with the impression or the illusion of oversight. Your drawings illustrate closeness, details and fine grain observations. In the narrow space of this exhibition, there is no way to see it all in one go. In fact, you have to look at it very closely.

These drawings draw an interesting comparison. The outcome of *tight* spaces is that you always end up in some form of negotiation. It forces you to rethink how you would do things, in the same way that you have to think carefully about how to look at the drawings in this exhibition.

Marika: It seems that part of the reasoning for doing this exhibition is to think about that idea of negotiation. It is all about negotiating sound, negotiating these 'Do not touch' or 'Do not talk' scenarios in these laneways. The laneway in the exhibition does feel like it could be a part of Melbourne.

Desirée: In Saigon, it is impossible to avoid interacting with a neighbour because of the narrowness of the space. It gives them a sense of belonging to the neighbourhood and the community. As Ho Chi Minh City develops and changes, people that once lived in these hẻms feel they have now lost this sense of community.

Taishin: It is important to remind ourselves that architects are not involved in these *super tight* urban situations and spaces like *hẻms* and narrow streets. Architects always seem to be on the side of demolishing these kinds of places. We have to find some methodology for dealing with *super tight* situations.

John: Architects often avoid working and designing in *super tight* urban and architecture conditions simply because it is quite difficult to deal with existing conditions and regulations.

Marika: One of the main challenges in designing in *tight* settings is the interaction between private property and public space. What is interesting about the one-room house proposition is the relationship between inside and outside is always present. You're always one space from the outside. In this way, the one-room house has an urban implication.

Taishin: The ideas of modernism are incredibly pervasive. We still think, 'this place is for drinking, that place is for sleeping.' We should be overlapping uses. For example, if we design the bathroom and bedroom in the same space, it can work! But before we even start, we refuse to believe it is possible. When space becomes *tight*, however, this process of negotiation and overlap becomes unavoidable. For example, in this bar, it becomes acceptable to drink on the stairs!

Desirée: This idea also happens in the *hẻms* where houses are generally built like little towers – one room over another one. Importantly, these rooms have multiple uses. But what makes this possible is time. At different times of the day, the room would have a different use. At night, the front of the house is where you store your motorbike when you go to bed. During the day, it's a shop, or it can be where you have a nap after having lunch.

Taishin: Ultimately, *tightness* is the generation of new overlapping spatial functions. I was surprised when I saw how tall and close together the high-rise apartment buildings are here in Melbourne. We don't have that kind of density in Tokyo. The buildings are so close to one another – you can almost reach out and touch the other building. I wonder what new functions could emerge from this situation. Maybe people can have a meeting between different buildings. *Tightness* has the power to create new situations.

room
ルランドの諺) 1559

33

Tight Density, Tight Familiarity, Overlapping City

Taishin Shiozaki
& Shiozaki Laboratory

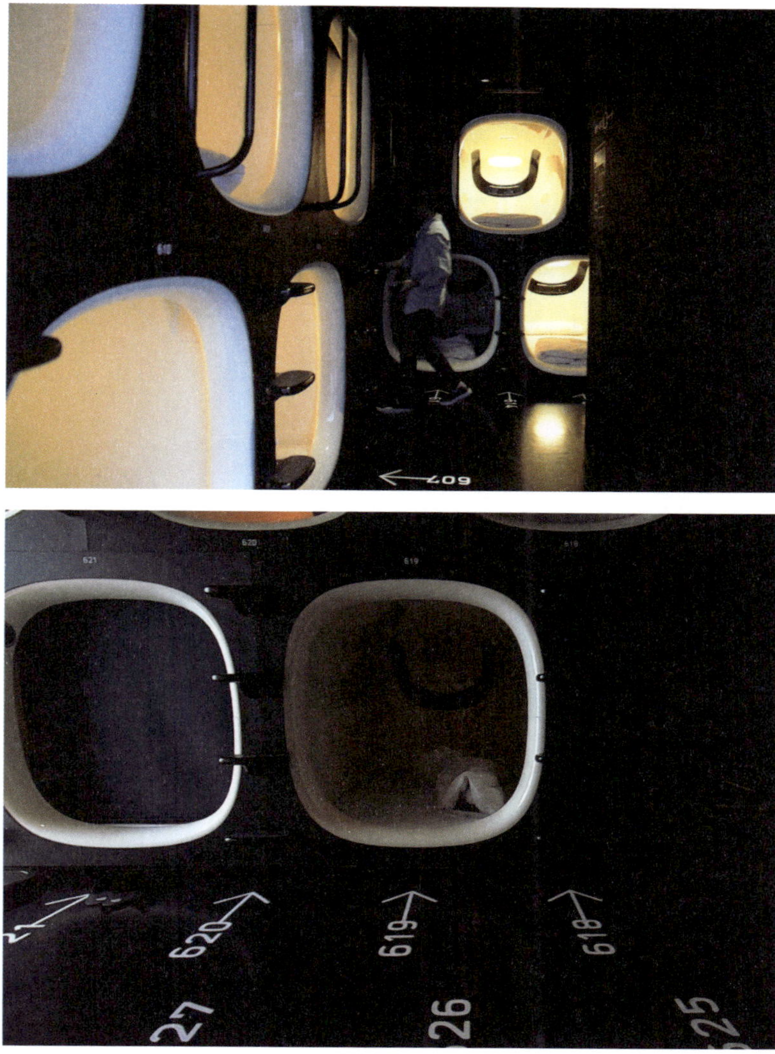

Tight Density, Tight Familiarity, Overlapping City is an original work by Taihin Shiozaki & Shiozaki Laboratory that explores scenes of everyday density in Tokyo. Capsule Hotel illustrates an example of an extreme form of formal compartmentalisation achieved through the reduction of a sleeping space down to the dimensions of the body.

カプセルホテル
Capsule Hotel

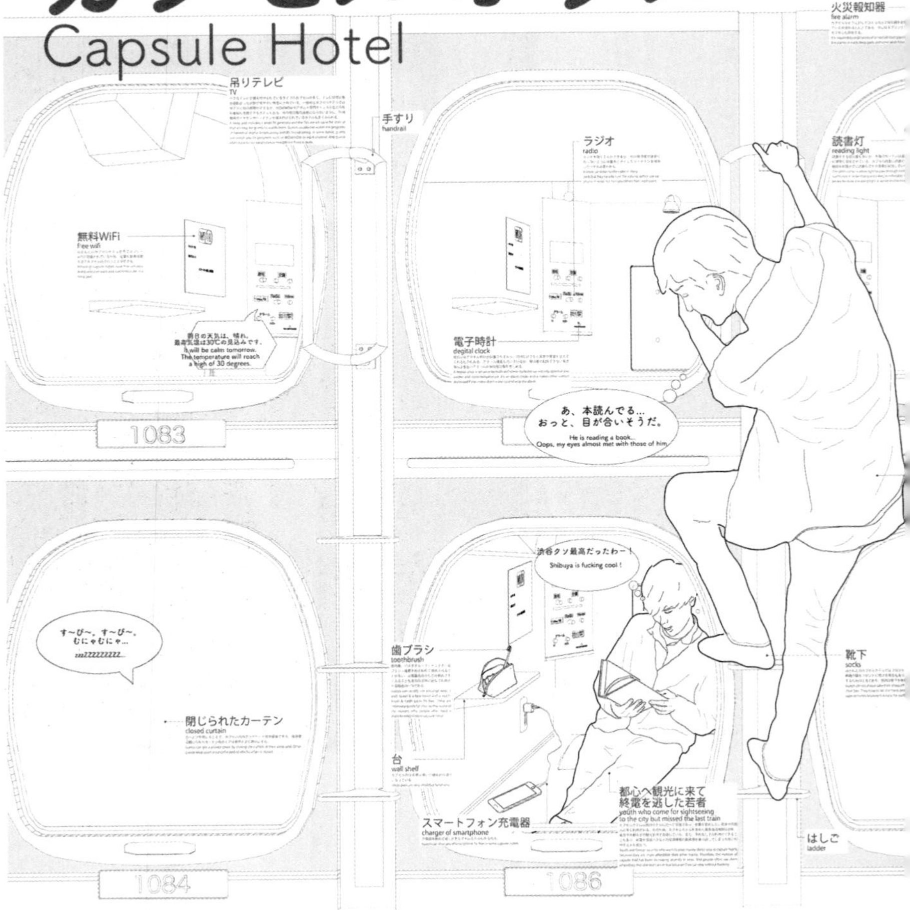

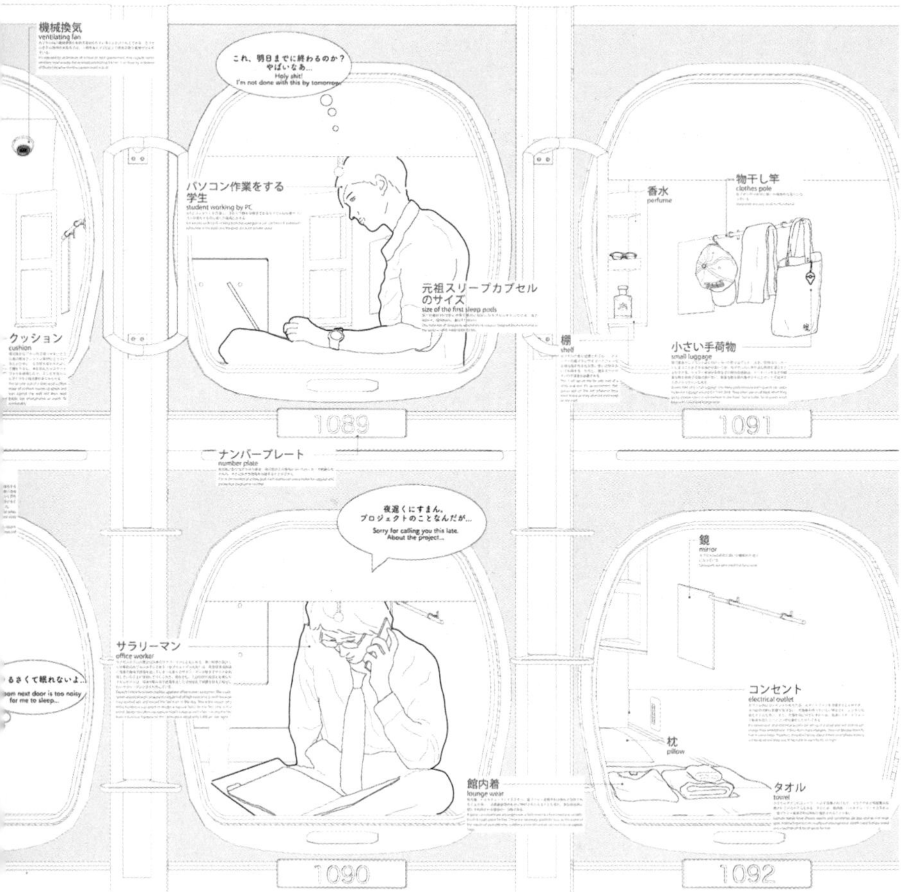
機械換気
ventilating fan
これ、明日までに終わるのか？
やばいなあ…
Holy shit!
I'm not done with this by tomorrow
パソコン作業をする学生
student working by PC
香水
perfume
物干し竿
clothes pole
元祖スリープカプセルのサイズ
size of the first sleep pods
クッション
cushion
棚
shelf
小さい手荷物
small luggage
1089
1091
ナンバープレート
number plate
夜遅くにすまん。
プロジェクトのことなんだが…
Sorry for calling you this late.
About the project…
鏡
mirror
サラリーマン
office worker
コンセント
electrical outlet
枕
pillow
館内着
lounge wear
タオル
towel
1090
1092

Nikon

9
10
GO!
560
5/15 川崎マイラーズ
トークショー
5.17~19
5.15 川崎マイラーズ
5 13. 14 15 16 17.
川崎競馬
伊豆の旅行が
Izuko
詳しくは
で検索

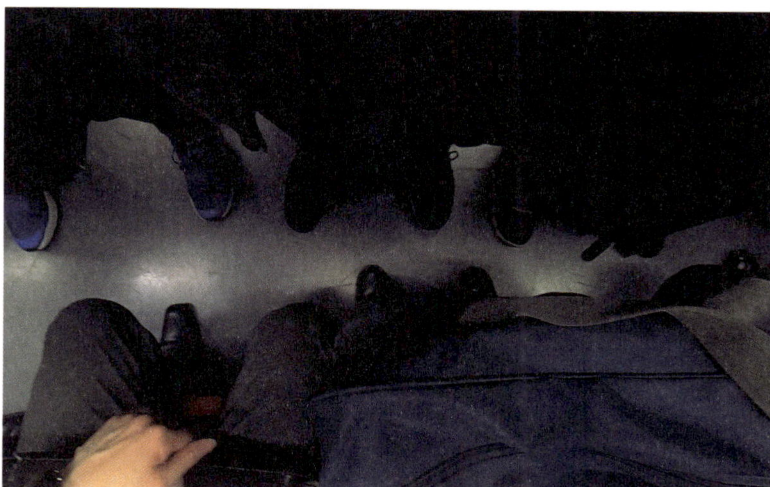

Rush House Train depicts the experience of the infamous morning commuter trains of Tokyo. These trains are arguably the most densely occupied urban spaces on the planet, so tight they require conductors to push commuters aboard and manually close the doors. This scene illustrates the series of behaviours that enable this to occur. This level of density can only be achieved through a high level of tolerance and social *tightness*, through adherence to agreed cultural norms.

満員電車
Rush Hour Train
新宿電波塔
Radio tower in Shinyuku
車内空調
air conditioner
車内放送
announcement
中吊り広告
hung advertising poster
Please set your mobile phone to the silent mode and refrain from talking on the phone.
音漏れ
sound leaking
車内案内表示装置
train signage
照明
light
向こうの電車は空いてるなあー
The opposite train is empty...
音漏れうるさっ！
That guy's music is loud. Be Quiet!
つり革
strap
触ってるって間違えられたらめんどくさぁ...
I don't want anyone to think I'm a groper.
I hate that she'll put her foundation cream on my clothes
こんなに近いの嫌だなぁ
Noooooo! It's too close to him.
痴漢冤罪防止の姿勢
position for preventing false molestation accusations
覗き込み
look into others
Yes! I can read his newspaper.
Shit!
暑苦しい～早く降りたいな...
Muggy. I wanna get off right now...
四つ折りの新聞
quarto newspaper
ポジション取り
positioning
本を読む小学生
elementary school student reading book
座席
seat
大きな荷物
large baggage
車椅子スペース
space for a wheel chair

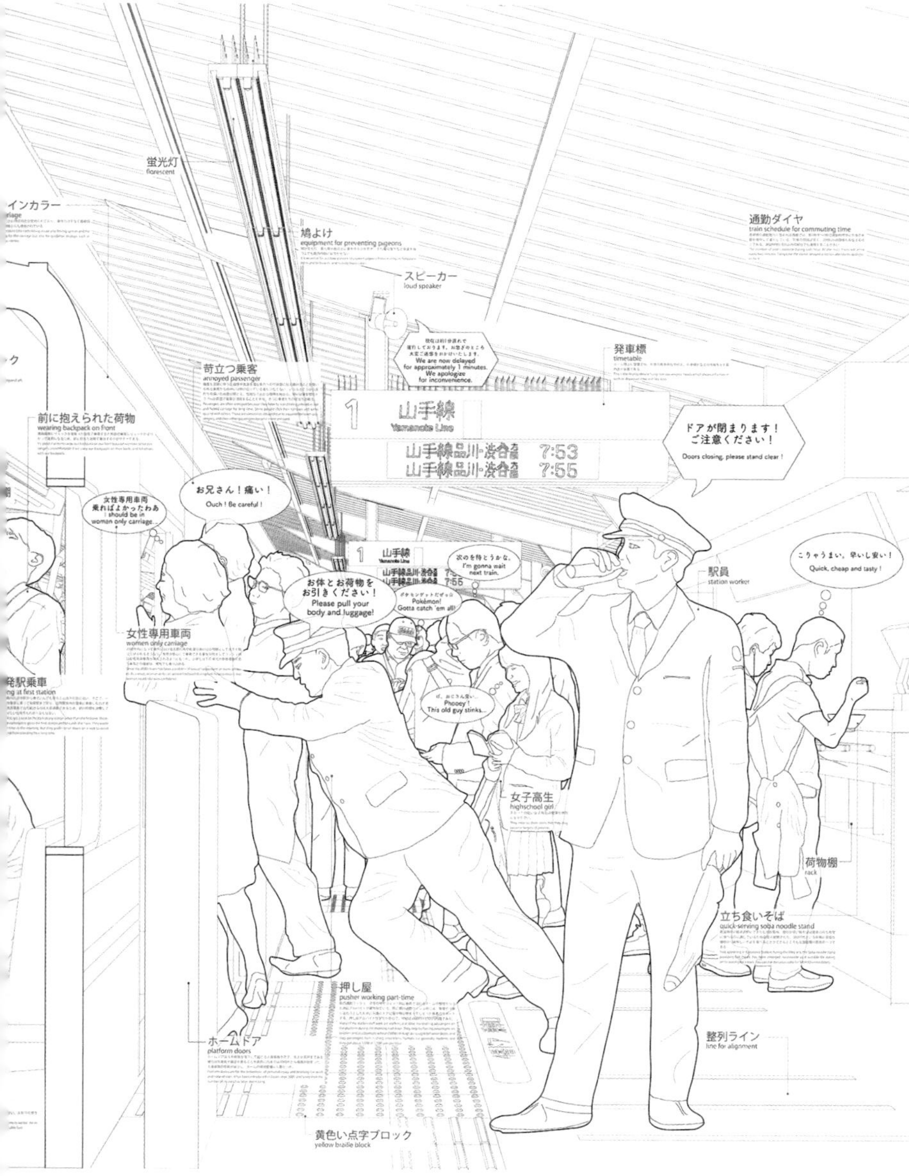
蛍光灯
florescent
インカラー
鳩よけ
equipment for preventing pigeons
スピーカー
loud speaker
通勤ダイヤ
train schedule for commuting time
We are now delayed
for approximately 1 minutes.
We apologize
for inconvenience.
発車標
timetable
苛立つ乗客
annoyed passenger
前に抱えられた荷物
wearing backpack on front
1 山手線
Yamanote Line
山手線品川・渋谷方面 7:53
山手線品川・渋谷方面 7:55
ドアが閉まります！
ご注意ください！
Doors closing, please stand clear !
女性専用車両
乗ればよかったわあ
I should be in
woman only carriage...
お兄さん！痛い！
Ouch ! Be careful !
次のを待とうかな。
I'm gonna wait
next train.
お体とお荷物を
お引きください！
Please pull your
body and luggage!
ポケモンゲットだぜッ
Pokémon!
Gotta catch 'em all!
こりゃうまい。早いし安い！
Quick, cheap and tasty !
駅員
station worker
女性専用車両
women only carriage
始発駅乗車
Phooey !
This old guy stinks...
女子高生
highschool girl
荷物棚
rack
立ち食いそば
quick-serving soba noodle stand
押し屋
pusher working part-time
ホームドア
platform doors
整列ライン
line for alignment
黄色い点字ブロック
yellow braille block

横丁
Pubs Area/YOKOCHO

混んできたなあ。
Wow. It seems to be crowded.
ホッピー
Hoppy
馬刺し
ホッピー
二階席
2nd floor seat
電飾看板
illuminated signboard
禁煙
禁煙
No Smoking
板前調理服
Japanese cook coat
桜
faked cherry blossom
ガスメーター
gas meter
外国人観光客
foreign visitors
はい！お待たせ！
Here it is !
狭いけど、なんかいい感じ！
So narrow space, but it feel so good!
げーっ。隣のおっさん近くて嫌なんだけど！
Eww, this old fart is too close !
へい！いらっしゃい〜！
How are you !
クールジャパン！
Japan is cool !
大将
master
もうフラフラじゃねえかよ（笑）
You're already staggering,Hahaha.
ここは何を食べても美味いなあ。
All of this izakaya's meals are delicious !
立ち飲み
TACHINOMI (standing bar)
又貸しシステム
Double layered lease system

Pubs Area / Yokocho provides an example of one of the many bar streets in Tokyo. Many of these neighbourhoods are hyper condensed. They are a by-product of Tokyo's urban metabolisation and made of small scale wooden buildings dating back to the first half of the twentieth-century.

Public Bath / Sento illustrates scenes from one of Tokyo's remaining sento or public bathhouses. Until recently it was common for neighbourhoods in Tokyo to have a communal bathhouse which residents would visit to bathe, relax and socialise. This scene illustrates the understanding of *tightness* as being a closeness or famialiarity amongst an urban community.

銭湯
Public Bath/SENTO

銭湯建築の様式
sento architecture style
あははは
Hahaha
ペンキ絵
painting
タイル絵
tile picture
顔見知り
people who knows each's face
あのじーさんまたおるわ。
I see that old man again today.
掛け湯
Kake-yu (pouring hot water on oneself)
でかいお風呂きもちいだろー？
Taking a large bath is relaxing, isn't it?
いい湯だ…
This feels good...
刺青
tattoo
シャワー
shower
なぁなぁ、シャンプーかして〜
Hey, can I use your shampoo ?
湯
hot water
おっけ〜
Yeah sure!
鏡
mirror
ロッカーの鍵
locker key
うん！
Yup!
マイシャンプー
one's own shampoo
カラン
taps
ケロリン桶
kerolin bowl

Cherry-Blossom Viewing documents a scene from the ubiquitous hanami parties that take place every year during spring in Japan. Cherry blossoms appear on the tree only briefly before they fall or are blown away by wind. It is a tradition to appreciate the blossoms with friends and colleagues. During the brief period that the blossoms appear the public gardens of Tokyo become full to bursting with revellers picnicing under the blossoms. This scene illustrates the temporal dimensions of *tightness*, that urban and architectural space can be both extremely *loose* and incredibly *tight* dependent on the movement of people, cultural, behaviour and event.

お花見
Cherry-blossom Viewing

提灯照明
lantern
枝折り禁止
No breaking a branch
インスタジェニック
ハイ、チーズ！
Are you ready? One, two, three!
まあきれい
Wow, it's beautiful.
Gentle! Don't tach them!
Great!
舞い落ちる花びら
falling petals
合コン
match making party
でしょ〜
I know, right?!
That's hilarious!
Hey, don't hold back.
新人歓迎会 & 送別会
welcome party & farewell party
ありがとうございます
Thank you.
He is boring.
Dam! He has his eyes on Chika.
Chika is so hot...
お酌
pouring alcohol for someone
日本酒
sake
プラコップ
plastic cup
リュック
bag
露店の食べ物
stall food
ブルーシート
blue plastic sheet

dynabook
docomo
Yodobashi-Camera
docomo
Yodobashi-Camera

ヨドバシカメラ
自転車を除く

Similar to the *Cherry-blossom Viewing* scene, *Location Based Game* documents the recent phenomena of augmented reality gaming. Using smart phones and GPS enabled tablets, games such as *Pokemon Go* have recast urban environments as gaming arenas. *Tightness* in this instance is generated through the sudden formation of a crowd of gamers in an otherwise sparesely populated area. *Tightness* is generated not only through the form of the urban environment but through social and cultural practices.

位置情報ゲーム

Location Based Game

噴水
fountain
ポケモンゲットだぜっ☆
Pokémon!
Gotta catch 'em all☆
Large display is
easy to see after all
タブレット
tablet
Shit!
They are in the way...
Yes !
A shiny pokémon appears !
お、卵かえった♡
Oh, I hatched an egg ♡
ピカチュウでちゅよ~
Look, sweetie. It's Pikachu.
Come out,
mythical pokémon...
Babble
イヤフォン
earphone
みんな、よく立ってできるな
I can't understand
why people play while standing
モバイルバッテリー
portable battery charger
自前の椅子
one's own chair

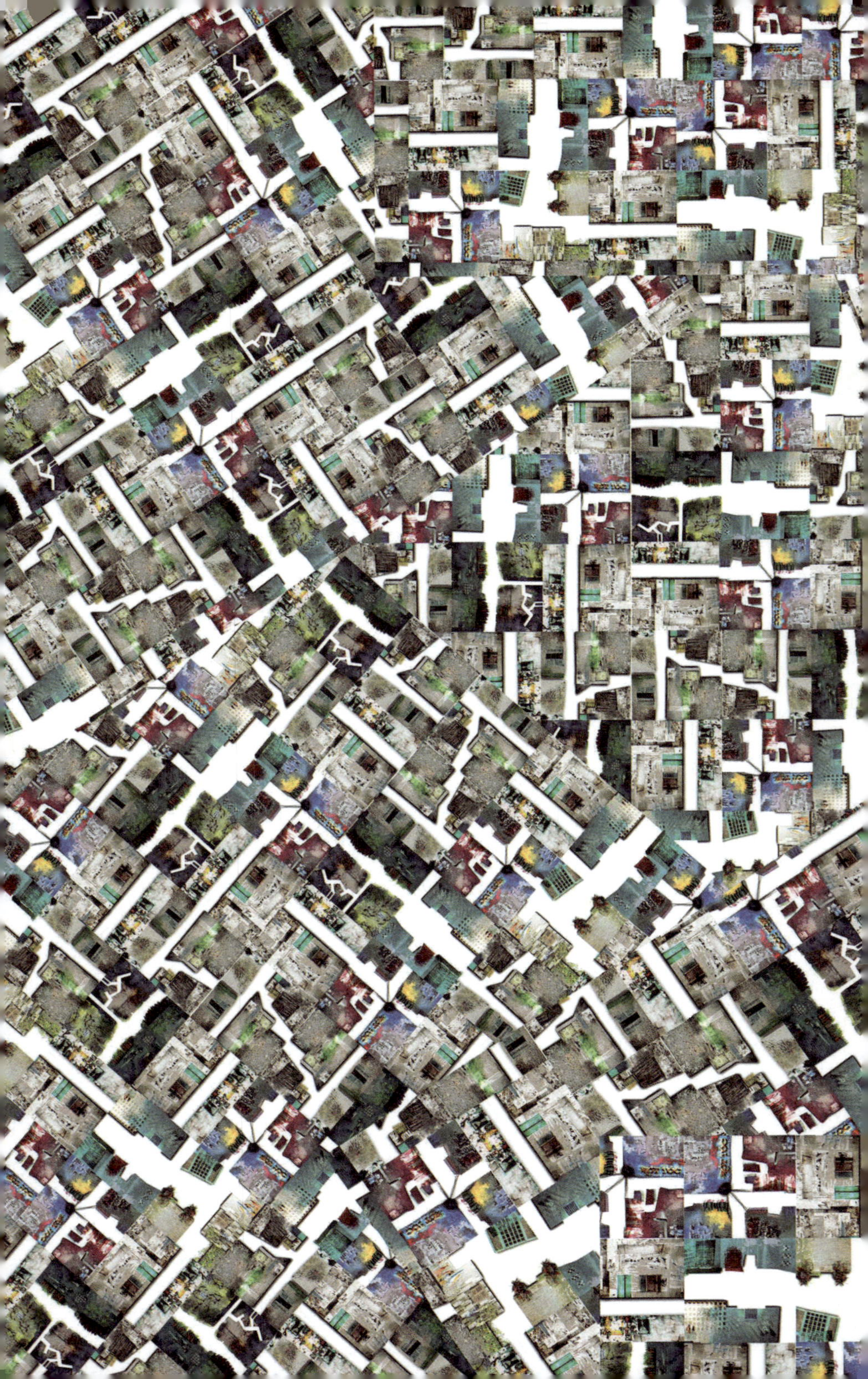

04

Mapas & Habitats Collage Series

Desirée Grunewald

Desirée Grunewald's body of work embodies the sensibility of a visual storyteller, and a cosmopolitan observer deeply invested in Vietnam's urban space. She has described the works as 'the creation of a collaged city made with the results of a rigorous taxonomy practiced on pictures of Vietnamese streets, defined by their narrowness and vernacular architecture.'

The collage techniques of Grunewald's work at times make this fictional city uncannily similar to the real thing.

Corridors is a series of works that emulates the experience of walking through a corridor inside a Saigonese alley. Different pieces extracted out of visual data from those streets are combined into a loop of new generated urban fields ad infinitum.

Detalles, is an intimate look into the rules of a *tight* urbanistic scenario through the lens of a close-up objective. Overlaps and non-defined thresholds may appear as an abstract composition where other ways of seeing highlight the urban overlooked.

The randomness of the page's shapes creates new collaged cities which opens up new territories for practice. The accumulation of pages adds a different reading where the sequence and order of the drawings are as important as each individual page. This book becomes a new site of propositional speculation and debate.

Pages from the *Transparent Book* show endless combinations of layered Saigonese alleys. It is through the accumulation of pages that spatial distance is achieved. The fracturing of space and discontinuity offers the potential for a different examination of a space.

35

A conversation with members of the Hẻms Archive Project based in Vietnam, Andrew Stiff and Thierry Bernard; Vietnam based photographer Sue Hajdu; Melbourne architect Ann Lau, and Desirée Grunewald, urban illustrator formerly based in Vietnam, now in Spain.

Graham: Let's pursue the differences between European cities and those in Vietnam. Certain parts of old cities seem to have a structure like the *hẻm*, yet the question is why it's persistent and pervasive in twenty-first century Vietnam and is it likely to continue?

Desirée: An old European town centre – the area that the government protects – seems much less chaotic than the *hẻms*, which are a collage of vernacular materials, chaotic movements and rhythms. Yet all of these qualities are not protected by the government for their heritage value to the city.

Andrew: Saigon is a city of two centres: a Chinese centre in Cho Lon and a more recent French colonial structure. These urban forms are all held and stitched together by a network of *hẻms*. You can see this network on Google Maps in the small towns of the Mekong Delta.

Thierry: Each house here in Saigon has the potential for commerce. They don't need a specific license for these activities – it's an individual decision. In Europe, you need a license to paint a shop. So, the division of private to public does not exist in Vietnam in the same sense. It brings a liveliness to social life.

Graham: So, that leads to *tightness* and your take on that term in relation to your body of work.

Desirée: I mostly use collage, and I realised that the *hẻms* are also intensely collaged. And how we occupy these spaces overlap – everybody is together, selling goods, working, taking naps or eating.

John: Overlapping is a term that Shiozaki uses to describe their work. It comes out of a particularly Japanese discussion.

Desirée: Yes, overlapping is spatial but also social. There might be a lady selling *ca phe sua da* with a baby next to someone sleeping in their living room while others are eating dinner and watching television. All of this is happening at the same time and is visible to the *hẻms*.

Andrew: The intense layering of uses in the *hẻms* is one of their distinguishing features. There is subtle partitioning: markets that appear in the morning and then at night are transformed into open-air events and street food vendors. The transitions in these spaces represent *tightness*. Everything is interconnected, and it moves in time with precision like clockwork.

Graham: It is interesting that you use the word precision. Some sociologists would describe Japanese culture as *tight* for its precise rules, conventions, and Vietnamese culture as *loose* for the opposite reasons. We have this strange perception that the *hẻm* is both chaotic and extremely precise.

Desirée: It's only chaotic when you're outside the flow. It's like traffic: once you're inside and running with the flow, it makes sense – it moves together and is precise.

Thierry: I have made several audio recordings with my equipment spaced about fifty metres apart along the *hẻm*. It's a bit like working with the present, past and future simultaneously. It also makes the sound very spatial.

Graham: Yes, you need to move through the sound before it is absolutely clear.

Desirée: You also observe the marks of different days, maybe months and years; posters posted over posters compressed into a kind of tightness of the texture in time.

Andrew: In my video work, I can only film a very tiny part of what is actually going on. So, it's an abstraction – you're conscious of 360 degrees worth of noise, movement, action, but the camera can only ever capture around 70 degrees.

Graham: You previously commented on your Saigon exhibition that the more conventionally documentary film seemed to resonate less with the inhabitants of the *hẻm* than the heavily layered abstracted images. This seemed more like realism to them.

Desirée: Sometimes the houses in the *hẻms* start being upgraded, growing vertically and merging at the top. They can't do it on the ground plane – it's like two trees, where the branches meet at the top.

Andrew: There isn't a master plan for the conditions we are describing. Ad-hoc additions to houses and infills often start with a bit of tarpaulin. Filling in a void over time is a sort of uncontrolled appropriation, but it's negotiated by the people that live there.

Desirée: It's a domestic way of finding solutions for a problem, a clever adjustment often without an architect.

Thierry: And all of this occurs in spaces that are extremely narrow, four metres and fifty metres long. It produces something strangely modern – like little Manhattan towers.

Andrew: As an architectural problem, you have a sort of Corbusian module with Vietnamese efficiency. Spaces have a tiny footprint, and everything is within arm's reach.

Graham: It's amusing to compare the tube house with Le Corbusier's Unite d'Habitation building because the proportion of those apartments are remarkably similar to a tube house. The sense of ownership is very different in these examples. Thierry, how does this compare to a city like Tokyo?

Thierry: In Tokyo, the government can't take over your house because they don't own it. But here, one can say, 'this is not your house anymore because of an urban master plan.'

John: In Tokyo, land ownership predates democracy. One of the first acts at the end of the feudal period was to enshrine the sovereignty of the individual landowner. So the city is fragmented. It is complicated when you hit boundaries, because you're dealing with two sovereign borders.

Andrew: In *Thu Thiem*, in District 2, a new development shifted around 14 000 residents. Those who had papers that documented their ownership were allocated land. Many people had been there for a lifetime; some had proof of ownership, others didn't, so one got a free house, and others got shipped out. In Phu Nhuan, just south of the airport, the government decided to widen the *hẻms* for car access. They paid people to give up two metres of their house and rebuild their front facade. The *hẻms* are now very different; they are straight with new gates to big villas sealed up and air-conditioned. So, it is an ecological disaster, as well as a social disaster.

Desirée: Yes, we value the *hẻms*, but the government doesn't.

Thierry: There is a view that the government is rebuilding the country and these issues will come later. (When it is already too late).

Graham: You described a vendor paying a homeowner for the space in a *hẻm* outside their house. Is this subletting their property? Is the *hẻm* publicly owned in any sense that we would understand it?

Andrew: The ownership of those spaces outside property seems to be more negotiated. I've been told its sometimes difficult for an outsider to arrive and set up street trading until they establish relationships.

Graham: Aside from nostalgia, is there any chance to build *hẻms* in contemporary Saigon?

Andrew: There is so much more vertical development in parts of Ho Chi Minh City, it is becoming similar to Singapore. Yet we also can't keep expanding cities. It doesn't work.

Desirée: The city is less traversable if it is expanded.

Andrew: People still want to live in Saigon. We should try to understand how these *hẻm* spaces manage density. Recently, some friends visiting from Singapore were blown away by the convenience of these spaces. Singapore has managed to erase so much of its older urban fabric, we should be learning from and encouraging these types of spaces in western cities.

John: The point is not just to value those qualities in Saigon, but to understand how it can be produced in new cities.

Graham: I was in Montpelier with a digital enthusiast who suggested that the old city had solved the question of not only timeless density, but of a beautiful, non-orthogonal geometry. He said, 'Of course, but obviously you can't build that again'. So there does need to be an algorithm for *tightness*?

Andrew: It's not necessarily that you want to rebuild that city, you want to rebuild those properties that made that such a successful space.

John: You want the performance of it.

Graham: But it is crucial to work out what ingredients are needed for the performance. What can you shed and what is essential?

Thierry: There is a kind of freedom in Vietnam. If there is material, for instance, I can build a shelter. Nobody will ask me to leave. I can't do that in Europe.

Desirée: You can't even sleep in your car in Europe.

Thierry: As the centre of District 1 becomes super expensive, many people are pushed into the suburbs – this is common around the world. But in that expansion, people can do what they want: they can choose to work where they live.

Desirée: When I tell someone I love the houses or the *hẻms*, they laugh and say, 'It's not beautiful, it's ugly'. It is difficult for me to explain why I find these spaces beautiful. I grew up in the western world with my own rules of privacy. I don't know if I can make the cultural shift.

Andrew: Many spaces in Vietnam's cities are run, organised, and maintained by the people that live in the *hẻms*. On paper there is a very strong government in Vietnam, and in Ho Chi Minh City, but the actual control of the government is very limited. Space is maintained and organised by the community and for the community, it forms its social support services.

People who move there have a period of adjustment where they're in the spaces and seen in the spaces. After this, they gradually make contacts and friends. Through those contacts, through those friends, they then get access to being able to rent a pitch in the markets.

The community then makes sure that people come to them, so the business of selling food in District 4, for example, is a shared experience. The lack of governments, law institutions, or control over what goes on, contributes to this feeling of *looseness* within this *tight* and dense space.

Sue: When I walk around photographing, I'm mainly considering my visual sense, but there is something else that is very prominent as you walk around these cities. That is the spatial sense of how you feel space shaping around you and forming around you.

Graham: There are so many urban instances of people in a small space with junk everywhere, and of finding some way of ordering that experience. This seems to be a way of contending with the *tightness* of the city. There is a calm orderliness to the city, even though lots of it is quite decrepit or chaotic.

Sue: Yes, I notice this, and I was particularly conscious of it in the image of the juice store with the big white wall in the background. The owner had neatly set up her oranges, cups, and things. To be able to run a business, you have to be able to accomplish a lot of things in a small amount of space without using too much energy in the heat, and without making too much of an impact on your environment.

Thierry: When you arrive in Vietnam for the first time, looking at the traffic, it looks like chaos. But, with some experience, you look to move through its flow, it's very organised. The arrangement itself is very organised. There is rarely an accident in such a chaotic environment. The sound of the city, it's noisy for an outsider, but people are respectful of each other. There are some hours that you know that they will stop and will not disturb the neighbourhood.

Ann: One of the things I have noticed over the last ten years, growing up in Hong Kong, is awareness of personal spaces and cultural gestures. Melbourne's transformation by the international student group is interesting – there is more diversity and acceptance of density. You have to negotiate your pathway with a much greater sense of awareness. Generally in the West, in Australia, we take up a lot of space. Most people grow up with a lot of space, and their awareness reflects that context.

Graham: Yes, and Melbourne's density is in floor area more than activity on the street. I want to bring the conversation back to the qualities of a city like Saigon. In terms of noise, it's not acceptable to talk loudly on your phone on a Tokyo train, for instance, but in Saigon, it's almost unacceptable to be quiet. I am curious how one finds respite or quietness in a city like Saigon.

Andrew: In terms of finding peace, there is peace in hearing noise, being surrounded by noise. It is reassuring. for anyone who lives in a city. When you go to the countryside, it's always slightly unnerving, because there is silence, and the sounds are unfamiliar.

Graham: Tsukamoto has been talking about the period of adjustment that needs to happen, regarding density. It isn't instant, and this happened incrementally in Tokyo, over generations. It's going to take a while for us to get used to that different scale of *tightness*.

Andrew: There are very valuable lessons in places like Saigon, Nha Trang, and Hanoi. They tell us how society can develop and change. In the West, we're so very focused on having our private space. How do we reconcile that with how we're going to need to live? Predictions are that by 2035, 75% of the world's population will be living in cities. We need to learn how to work with that, and ask, how can the city change to accommodate these numbers in a sustainable way?

Graham: Perhaps the question is what we learn from cultures that have reconciled themselves to much greater density. Instances where *tightness* is not uncomfortable.

36

Hẻm & Pha Lau Video Works

Andrew Stiff

This series of video works was made by Andrew Stiff between 2016 and 2019 through observation and recording of one part of District 4 in Ho Chi Minh City. Over years and many visits, Stiff built up an archive of video material of daily life in this particularly intense and labyrinthine part of the city. Once known for its crime and poverty, and closed to foreigners, this island created by canals across from the colonial centre of District 1, is in the flux of development and gentrification. The title *Hẻm* refers to the layered network of *tight* lanes that cross the whole district and much of the city. *Pha Lau* refers to the soup made from beef offal, with a rich red colour which can be seen in large open pots throughout the area.

A wide range of digital filters are used to process the raw imagery, abstract it, and test the visual language of the urban environment. The techniques measure its recognition and capture or amplify its qualities through partial abstraction. Blurring techniques, as well as overlays and extrusions aim to focus on urban details or capture the fleeting and ephemeral nature of urban life in District 4.

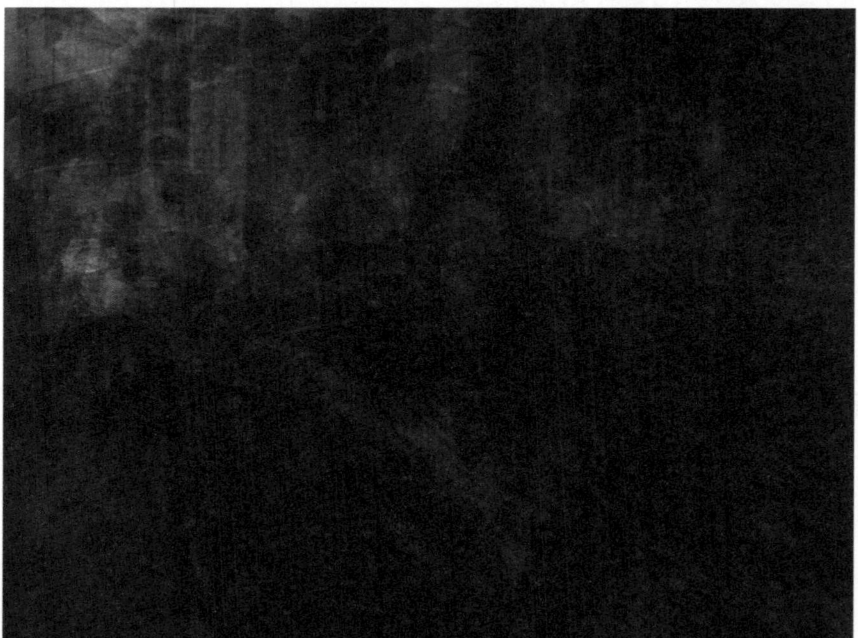

The intense abstraction in the moving image rejects straightforward documentary and throws focus on motion in the space, the passing of time and the strong elision of objects. The stills take on a painterly quality which belies the sense of immersion in the city's transitory experience.

ĐIỆN LẠNH TẬN NHÀ
PEPSI

Often the camera is left motionless in the urban space for many hours, sometimes on the ground – a literal street view or passive observer of the street, and its ordinary events. Some of these record the exceptional changes of use in a smal space over the course of a day; others record the rhythms of negotiating a tiny plot of urban territory in the daily business.

37

Production in Tight Cities

Productive landscapes are a by-product of urban density and the *tight* city, and are often unseen through the urban lens. The relationship of urban density to the broader collection of agricultural landscapes that support cities is conceptually part of the *super tight*. The possibilities for folding these rural hinterlands back into the urban core is relevant to its agenda.

The Super Tight project has primarily focused on forms of urban occupation and the *tight* city as an object. However, a key discussion during the project's development and an exhibition forum, centred around a video work by Dr Alban Mannisi, Associate Professor Charles Anderson and Dr Yazid Ninsalam from RMIT University's Landscape Architecture programs. The film entitled *Hokkien Mee Diplomacy* (2019) documented the relationship between the dense urban environments of Singapore and the market gardens of Johor located across the Johor Strait in Malaysia.[1] This work, and its accompanying research, offered a useful counterpoint to others in the exhibition. It depicts the vast peri-urban hinterland that exists on the Malaysian peninsula which supports the extreme population density and urbanisation of Singapore. This work, and its discussions, suggest that urban density cannot be separated from the supporting landscapes which are largely hidden from those cities.

If the *super tight* is focused on the space inside cities, its consequence is equally present on the outside landscapes that support them. While architects focus on the dense centre of cities and their organisation, occupation and formal characteristics, we often overlook the vast peripheral hinterland that supports dense urban cores. Cities such as Singapore and Hong Kong, both of which feature in the Super Tight exhibition, are in many ways models of the physical and social management of extreme density. Yet both cities rely heavily on supply chains that stretch well beyond their administrative borders.

Dense and compact cities are generally agreed to be more environmentally sustainable than sprawled settlements. There is a correlation between increased levels of urban density, close proximity of employment and amenities, and a reduction in the overall carbon footprint of a city. Smaller and more consolidated building footprints suggest fewer resources are required to build and service a city on a per capita basis.[2] Likewise, a smaller urban footprint increases the efficiency and viability of mass transport systems and urban walkability. A similar outcome is observed when one reviews the overall ecological footprint of dense cities. Ecological footprint, measured as global hectares (gha), is the land area required to support total urban consumption. Per capita, dense cities perform better overall than the nations that contain them.

New York City for example, has an annual consumption of 6.1 global hectares per person. The national average for the United States is 8.1 gha. This rate difference is not universal, but it is common in developed countries.[3]

As cities increase in population, scale and affluence, so does the ecological footprint or land area required to support their consumption. Scale and population density lead to efficiencies relative to that population. In large cities, however, the vast hinterland and supply chain that supports them is exaggerated. This condition is particularly relevant in the discussion of the super dense or *tight* city. Dense cities tend to have a disproportionately large ecological footprint relative to the actual physical footprint. For example, metropolitan Melbourne is the densest city in Australia but sparse by global standards, with an ecological footprint of 6.8 gha.[4] New York City has a comparable footprint per capita, but a substantially higher level of density.[5] The consolidation of a population affects the proportion of hinterland area to the city limits. Consequently, Melbourne requires approximately 38 times its urban footprint to support itself. New York City, by contrast, consumes 1441 times its footprint.[6]

Urban density is maintained by displacing production, particularly food production, elsewhere. The increase in population density is not matched proportionally by the hinterland footprint, exaggerating the invisible footprint of the dense city. For cities like Melbourne, can this productive hinterland be absorbed within its physical boundary? This shadow footprint phenomenon is exaggerated in city-states that do not have the productive capacity to support themselves. In an era of global trade, it is accepted practice that a large percentage of the materials and energy that support cities is sourced abroad. However, with cities like Hong Kong and Singapore, almost all of the productive landscape that supports them has been displaced, all around the world.

The ecological footprint of Singapore is 5.9 gha per capita, but it has a biocapacity of approximately 0.04 gha per person.[3] Again, almost all the energy and resources consumed in the city are imported. A similar relationship is evident across the border, where much of the state of Johor and the south-eastern Malaysian peninsula provides agricultural resources for Singapore. This relationship has changed in recent years with a decline in agricultural productivity and inflationary pressures in Malaysia, particularly, fresh food and perishable goods. Hong Kong has 0.03 gha of productive land, a similar productive capacity deficit to Singapore. Hong Kong can rely on mainland China for many of its resources, particularly power and water. Despite increasing integration between the two systems, there is a persistent issue of food security in the city. Hong Kong imports more than 90% of the food that is consumed in that city.[7]

About a third of this supply comes from mainland China, however, the remainder is sourced from overseas. The United States of America and the European Union account for another third, with food often travelling more than 11,000km. There is a substantial environmental cost associated with sourcing food and resources from the other side of the world. Global shipping is one of the major transport sector contributors to greenhouse gases. The dislocation of a city from its productive hinterland cultivates an *out of sight out of mind* consumption attitude.

Social behaviours, expectations and rates of consumption play a role in the environmental footprint of cities. There is a clear correlation between the affluence of nations and their ecological footprints, regardless of density. For example, New York and Ho Chi Minh City are the largest cities of their respective countries and major commercial centres. New York City's density is more than twice that of Ho Chi Minh City. Despite this, the ecological footprint of New York City is more than 3.5 times that of Ho Chi Minh City. The gains afforded by tighter urban environments are offset by what Michele Gelfand has described as *loose* cultural frameworks and associated patterns of consumption.[8] That is, the individual freedoms of affluence prioritised in a *loose* culture may mitigate against the dense built fabric of an affluent city. *Tightness*, as we have described in the Super Tight exhibition, seeks to link the built environments and the behavioural patterns of urban life.

Tightness is a cultural and social practice that contributes to reducing a city's urban footprint. This logic must also foster a culture of *tight* consumption in which dense settlement is brought together with production frameworks and the resources required to sustain them. To cultivate a culture of *tight* consumption, a city must be coupled to its productive hinterland. A dense city might take this idea further and fold its productive zones into its overall form.

The technical limitations to this proposition are closely bound to the history of modernity. During the previous two centuries, cities invested in infrastructure projects that moved the productive networks of cities beyond their boundaries. Water supply, waste removal and power generation were distributed from hinterlands to the centre of cities. This marker of urban development remains incomplete for a substantial percentage of the world's urban population without running water, waste management or electrical power.

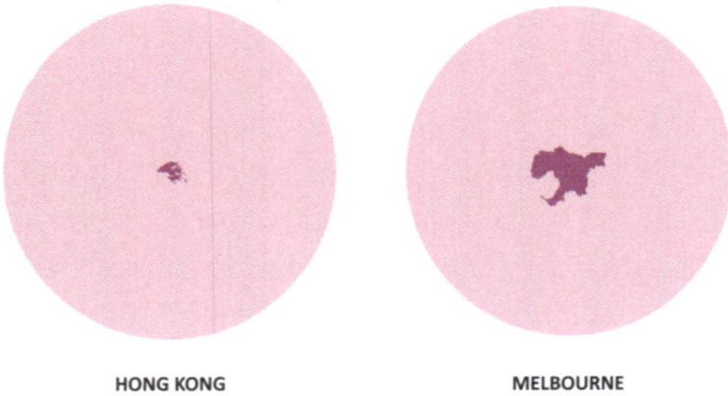

Comparison of urban footprint
vs global hinterland

Anderson, Ninsalaam
& Manissi
Hokkien Mee
Diplomacy Johor

Graham Crist
Demonstrations 2018
Ho Chi Minh City

However, more recently, there are trends towards models that source electricity in a distributed manner, and water locally. As these measures unfold and accelerate, they will impact the relationship between cities and the hinterlands. These are largely technical solutions that can begin to reframe the conceptual understanding of a city and its footprint boundary.

In order to fold cities and their productive landscapes into one another, it is necessary to reconsider the planning regimes that underpin them. In particular, the concept of single-use or Euclidean planning approaches that separate productive land from a city centre can be unwound. Historically, the separation of urban functions, in particular, populations from manufacturing, was for the purpose of public health, and with real benefits. The logic of the healthy garden city providing clean air and water had parallel motivations for segregating urban functions. New technologies and standards of goods, materials and food manufacturing have allowed for a reconsideration of this separation.[9]

Globally, there are trends toward the reintegration of manufacturing as a component of high-density urban cores. The *Vertical Urban Factory* project led by Nina Rappaport has documented examples of high-density urban manufacturing facilities and precincts.[10] This research argues for the vitality and importance of urban manufacturing as both a driver of environmental and social sustainability. The advantages of integrated production-consumption cities has been exaggerated by the ongoing COVID-19 pandemic. The privileges for those who can work and source their goods locally over those reliant on commutes and supply chains has amplified inequalities.

Two speculative design research projects carried out at the RMIT University School of Architecture & Urban Design explore the return of urban manufacturing and production, and how this could contribute to the *tightening* of already dense cities.

Making Vietnam focussed on manufacturing cultures in Vietnamese cities, in particular, Ho Chi Minh City. Over the past thirty years, there has been a dramatic change in Vietnamese urban manufacturing, which has coincided with the arrival of international capital and the development of global manufacturing centres in designated special economic zones.[11] Since 1990, the density of Ho Chi Minh City has halved as it follows western development patterns. The project sought to integrate factory manufacturing with dense urban fabric, both in use patterns and urban form. It examined techniques for integrating big box urban objects with the fine-grain lived fabric of Vietnamese cities. These cities have a strong culture of intricate density and small-scale workshop manufacturing.

RMIT Architecture
Making Vietnam
Saigon

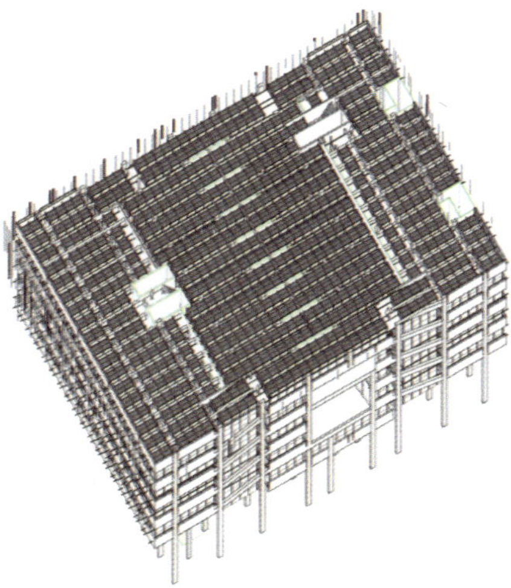

RMIT Architecture
FarmHD
Hong Kong

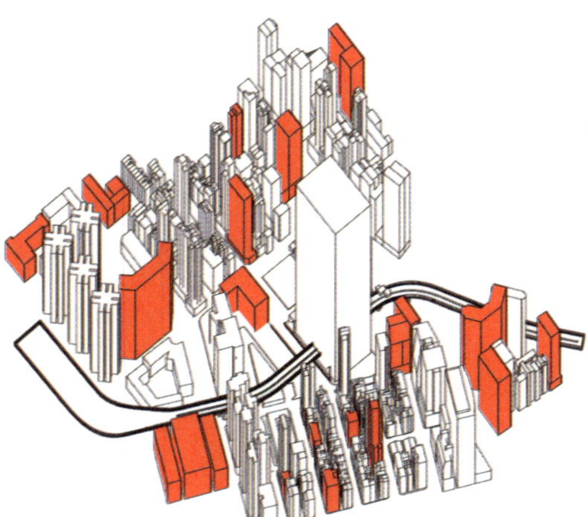

RMIT Architecture
FarmHD
Hong Kong

Vietnam's economic growth has seen the rise in factories built for export industries divorced from the urban fabric and the domestic economy. This condition has had implications for both the city and its peripheral hinterland.

The *Making Vietnam* project identified three existing urban types: *tube* housing, the industrial shed and the informal shack. These types were designed into three urban models. Firstly, the *Wall Court* model, a *tube* housing block rotated relative to the street, that screened private space from the adjacent industry. Secondly, the *Big Roof*, an open shed that accommodated and unified diverse functions into the dense fabric. And finally, *Street Teeth*, a model for small scale buildings that stitch set back industrial buildings into the surrounding streets. These models were applied and tested on sites in Ho Chi Minh City's District 5 and Binh Dang District as prototypes for *tightening* the industry and city relationship as well as the connections between the metropolis and the hinterland.

FarmHD explored the relationship between dense cities, the food supply chains that support them and design-led strategies for the reintegration of food production. The project focused on Hong Kong as an urban case study of extreme density and significant food security challenges.[12] A series of speculative design proposals were developed that sought to capitalise on latent opportunities within the city's urban fabric to enable future high-density urban farming economies.

One proposal explored the potential for repurposing multilevel car parking structures in the city. Despite efficient and heavily used mass transport systems and a largely walkable footprint, Hong Kong has over 690,000 designated car spaces.[13] The design proposal explored a future scenario in which the large-scale adoption of autonomous vehicles has drastically reduced the need for car parking, creating a large amount of redundant built space in the city. Most car parking structures are not designed for human occupation, and few are easily adaptable for habitable programs such as apartments or office space. At the same time, demolishing and rebuilding these buildings would require a significant waste of carbon, both in existing and future embodied energy costs.

High-intensity factory food growing uses less water, no pesticides and is up to twenty times more efficient than conventional agriculture. As the system requires no daylight, it is ideal for repurposing the deep plans of underutilised car parks. Through the *Farm HD* project, a model of adaptive reuse was developed that took advantage of existing concrete structures, repurposed to pack together a hyper-dense structure of plant growing bed modules.[14]

Testing this model on a car park structure in Kowloon, we found that eight storeys of car parking could accommodate enough growing modules to produce approximately ten tonnes of edible leafy greens per day. This is enough to provide the daily vegetable intake of an entire neighbourhood, even in the extreme density of Kowloon. If we extrapolate this across all the car parking structures of Hong Kong, this suggests an urban model in which a substantial percentage of the city's daily food requirements could be produced locally within existing building stock.

The implications of such a move for cities are significant. As it becomes even more practical to grow and produce goods within the city, new models of architecture and urban design could emerge that allow for new building typologies that are unoccupied by people but instead set aside for the making and growing of things. Cities and their infrastructures are responsible for more than two-thirds of global carbon emissions. While many mechanisms to mitigate climate change are beyond the domain of architecture and urban design, the tightening of our cities and especially the goods which supply them is one of the greatest contributions we can make. It is not enough to build dense urban cores as places to live and work. We must consider a future in which cities integrate all the elements of their production-consumption cycle within a *tight* urban culture, and with a *tight* metropolitan / hinterland boundary.

38

Hokkien Mee Diplomacy

Charles Anderson, Alban Mannisi
& Yazid bin Ninsalam

Hokkien Mee Diplomacy is an original film exploring the relationship between the *tight* urban environment of Singapore and the market gardens of Johor, located across the Straits of Johor in Malaysia. These dense productive landscapes provide food, cut flowers and other fresh produce for consumption in Singapore. The film suggests that urban density is frequently a site of consumption, and that many of the world's densest cities are fully reliant on a productive hinterland outside of their metropolitan or national boundaries to exist. The film documents the environmental consequences of this approach in Johor.

39

A conversation with landscape architects Alban Mannisi, Katrina Simon, Yazid bin Ninsalam and Charles Anderson.

Alban: There is insufficient space for agriculture in Singapore. It relies on Malaysia for agricultural production. As a consequence of this arrangement, Singaporeans don't see their food being grown and don't see the effects of the city's density.

Intensive agriculture has destroyed the quality of life for people living in parts of Malaysia. These people work in what could be called a food forest which is itself a form of density. They use very small amounts of land to produce large amounts of vegetables.

Through our work we are trying to prove that there is a possibility in Singapore to combine urban density with environmental density. We can feed a society within the urban environment through urban farming.

The *Edible Garden City* project reintroduces local plants back into Singapore as a means of changing how we see the landscape – as being something more than ornament. However, this is not in line with the policy of the government. The maintenance is too complicated. People can produce food in Singapore, but it's not considered a priority.

Yazid: In south-east Asia, countries have to depend on those neighbouring them. From an economic point of view, it's about breaking up the value chain. Malaysia has land and we depend on them to be able to grow food for production.

Charles: Singapore is also trying to push its technology capability. It can bring about the possibility of food production through vertical farming and indoor farming.

Katrina: Singapore has a very strong identity as a garden city due to its existing landscape. It's extremely lush and beautifully kept, however, only a particular type of plant is accepted.

Charles: During the project, we were told that if you want to set up an organic farm, it has to be as far away as possible from industrial farming due to the pesticides. In contrast, in the Cameron Highlands, it isn't possible to establish an organic farm, although they want them. You can't do it because they're always going to be close to industrial-scale farming.

Graham: Unfortunately, the logic appears to be that nature's too messy to be in a *tight* city. When agriculture is in the city, not as many toxins can be used as out in the invisible hinterlands. Everyone will see them in a factory belching pollution in the middle of the city. But at the same time, you can't have the natural messiness of rotting vegetables on compost and insects.

Charles: In Singapore, they are growing a western diet and have forgotten the local foods that thrive in those environments very successfully. These don't require the number of herbicides, pesticides and coverings that strawberries require. One of the discoveries in Singapore was that a lot of the grassroots movements are about rediscovering what their original foods were and could be again.

Yazid: There has always been a debate around whether you're blessed or burdened to live in the tropics. On the one hand, everything grows quickly and having tall skyscrapers is also a luxury. The question is, how do you manage and maintain this greenery within such a *tight* space?

Charles: In the Cameron Highlands, we're growing food that should be grown in temperate zones, and it's destroying the tropical rainforest. Again, the geopolitical struggle is around the power of the temperate zone climates imposing their urban and agricultural models on parts of the world that actually shouldn't be functioning in that way.

Yazid: We ran an event where we invited food producers, people interested in food from a social science perspective or designers. They shared a couple of projects that they have been doing in Singapore and around the region. One of the responses we've seen towards not having enough space or having to work in *tight* locations is to use vertical farming typologies.

I'm glad that they are not going in that direction. They were looking at more conscious markets or more conscious end users, stakeholders, clients who are keen and open to small agricultural projects in their own spaces. We have seen this in the schools, where students can learn about the importance of growing food. Having that proximity to farming from an early age begins this conversation about where our food comes from and how we maintain it. It takes time, maintenance, and lots of space and knowledge to cultivate food for a city.

40

A conversation with the RMIT Design Hub Gallery Super Tight curators, Kate Rhodes and Nella Themelios

Nella: Let's begin the discussion by reflecting on the exhibition, on both its conceptual and formal or experiential qualities.

John: The broader context of the Super Tight research is urbanism and density in cities. In contrast to other work in this area, we were keen to make Super Tight focus on questions of design and the role of designers in these issues. We needed to be able to do that in a physical way and to explore that through design speculation. The starting point was an interest in a particular approach and attitude to cities in Asia. As the proposition formed around this question of the *supertight*, it became necessary for us to test that at scale.

Graham: When we think about urban density as a problem of spatial design, its questions are reliant on full scale perception of geometry and figuration of those spaces. The exhibition is drawn from our lived experiences of cities and particular spaces. It transposes these spaces into new architectural propositions.We have been to Shibuya's Tight Bar, but it was described to me before I experienced it for myself. So, we have both been inside the *real* version of this bar and transposed the ideas into the space we are sitting in now. The question of the transposition and the level of abstraction experienced was important.

Kate: It helps to answer some of the problems associated with bringing design into the gallery. For example, here in the gallery, the design object is separated from its function in the world. We then try to build our way into functionality or the experience of spaces and objects. If you hand me a drink, I get to perform what exactly happens in the real bar.

John: The way we've tackled this comes from our understanding that the form has a performative role in the city – you can't separate cities from form and scale. We had to determine how little of the original was needed to replicate the performance of the spaces we've identified as being important.

Nella: How important were design processes like sampling in developing the installations?

Graham: We are more interested in the processes – the evolution more than its origins. But we needed to engage with the gallery space and also bounce against the city. The word intimacy kept coming up as what we were trying to produce, but we also identified this quality in those cities we like. There is something about sitting in extremely close quarters with people – it has a social dimension. A couple of years ago, there was apparent anxiety in Melbourne about density and high-rise buildings. As development started exploding, we heard the question: Do we want to become Hong Kong? For us, we thought the answer to this question was: why not? Concern about vistas, human scale, those biases in the western city against density interested us. How do you prise apart density and poverty or overcrowding? Those nineteenth-century biases linger in the conversation.

Kate: Do we have a fear of gathering and social connection?

John: We've never attempted to diagnose the fear. We have an optimistic view of density and how the positive aspects can be a valuable counter-argument. There is a small house movement and the small footprint movement. However, we sit on the precipice of a global environmental catastrophe. But tiny houses or medium density are window dressing. We need to take a broader and more ambitious view of density. At a macro level, land use is complicit in the impact that cities have on carbon emissions and climate change. One of the most sustainable things we can do is live closer together. Not just in medium scale pot plant-filled warehouses but densely populated.

Graham: The question is, what can we do as designers of the built environment? Climate change is a colossal issue, and there are a hundred strategies that need to be taken. What can we most effectively do for it? The biggest thing that affects a building's carbon footprint is its physical square metres.

Nella: There is a section of Shiozaki Lab's drawing of a packed train where a guy has a thought bubble saying, 'I hope people don't think I am a groper'. Recent discussions around the design of cities have drawn attention to how they allow some identities to exist and others not. The majority of the train network users, for instance, are probably women, and they are not involved in designing these very *tight* spaces.

Graham: That is a very interesting observation and one that hasn't come up so far in these talks. It goes straight to a whole cluster of connotations of density and its relationship to safety in cities. You're right, these are issues that affect women more than men. On the flip side is the low-density suburban city, which has been an instrument to control women and keep them in a 'safe' domestic space. More broadly, is a high-density city more equitable than a low-density city? It depends. If you compare Saigon with Hong Kong, they have very different profiles of inequality.

Kate: So does density make us more powerful? Does it make our ability to gather easier, to talk, to collectively make change?

Graham: I've previously tried to organise a student demonstration in Perth, a car-dominated city. It isn't easy to demonstrate and gather when you have to get bussed to the location as opposed to pouring out of your apartment into the street. So there are practical issues, but the question of control and freedom and how they relate to urban design and density is complicated.

John: In the cities we have looked at for this project, there are different versions of what Graham is describing. In Saigon, control seems pretty limited, but at the same time, nobody owns the land or the right to gather. Conversely, buildings are *tightly* controlled in Tokyo, but they're the private domain of the individual.

Graham: *Tightness* ultimately tries to reconcile freedom with closeness.

TOA

Towards a Supertight City

What kind of place is the *supertight* city? What could we conclude from the concrete examples of cities in Asia, or on the many speculations and the numerous conversations which surround them?

The Super Tight project methodologically pursued the real rather than the true, evidence rather than proof. That is, it sought to show instances of cities working and some of the experiences of being in those places. That is not a doctrine or a set of policies of how cities are or should always be. It aims for neither forecasts nor trends, but asks simply `what if'? What if a *supertight* city could be desirable, and what we could direct that desire at reducing our urban footprint?

The works shown in this book employ techniques of observation to produce new knowledge of the city. By surveying and gathering often ordinary events and behaviours, images begin to emerge of what we mean when we use the word *tight* to describe a city. Desirée Grunewald's collages, or Archie Pizzini's photographs, for example, both conduct surveys that are neither entirely exhaustive nor complete - the social sciences and conceptual art practices overlap. At another scale, Tsukamoto's early publications with Atelier Bow Wow show us another example of the impulse to map and to record. Where Pizzini's works captured inhabited traces of the urban, the well known axonometric drawings from the Pet Architecture or Made in Tokyo series survey the concrete equivalent in buildings. In each of these three examples, there exists a concern for capturing the many scales of what we have identified as *tightness*. It could be a behaviour, an arrangement of furniture or a characteristic common to a society. What these each have in common is that they are fleeting or briefly, defined. Because they are fragmentary and specific it makes it difficult for us to regulate, capture or to re-create in other settings. They tend toward the informal.

These observations suggest that a key way to bring about change in the contemporary city is through the design of the individual project. For those in urban policy, the project is described as demonstrative of a framework. In this research we might hope that it sounds more like innovation of a prototype, and an adjustment of a working city. In the talks and interviews of this book, we hear the struggles with this challenge. The masterplan is no longer appropriate or suitable for the task. The Super Tight project did not set out to create policy or construct a theory. Rather it hoped to broaden how we talk about density in cities such as ours in Melbourne, or elsewhere. Through the design and observational work exhibited and published here, it hoped to capture positive experiences of high density cities.

Perhaps as the most tangible approach to the *supertight* understood as an urban adjustment, we are left with the individual dwelling, or even the single room. It is here that the architects in this publication seem most comfortable to speculate. So many proposals for a *tight* city occur at this scale- the *tight* dwelling inserted deftly into the city. Tokyo is a supreme example of this, and the remarkable design culture emerging in Vietnam has also drawn on this legacy.

The Shiozaki Lab elaboration of the overlapping city though a precise diagramming of urban imprecision, is critical to drawing out qualities of the *supertight*. It opens up a dialogue about a Tokyo urban culture viewed as *tightly* disciplined, and gently exposes the gross inefficiency of zoning in modern western cities. It is hardly a new idea for urban places that re-program daily, and just as importantly, it does not require radical shifts in how we occupy buildings or cities. It is a pursuit of the clues that architecture can give to this urban overlapping; of an architecture and a city that is more robust, and capable of accommodating change toward super-dense inhabitation.

In almost all of the talks and interviews made for Super Tight, the conversations conflate the physical experience of a city with the lifestyles it supports. Several of the works use maps, diagrams and collage to capture the qualities of both. How we document density, how we image it might provide us with clues for how to reconstruct it in another context, separate from the local conditions that initially supported it.

The conversations also wrestled with the word 'tight', to keep it from meaning small or diminutive. Its dimension is merely a by-product of a kind of precision achieved through negotiation. To reach mutual agreement, cohabitation, requires us to work with what is at hand. It is a kind of ad-hoc resourcefulness that has been described by Pizzini as *rasquachismo*. But why do compromised resources necessarily equate to a *supertight* outcome? Roland Barthes' essay Packages (from Empire of the Signs), describes Japanese gestures and objects as being framed. Precision is constructed by the object or gesture stopping or finishing; delimiting itself from its surroundings. We find this in Tsukamoto's description of Tokyo's suburbs and how the houses are framed by one metre wide external gaps. This occurs in Seoul too. This framing does not limit sharing, rather in order to share in an object or behaviour, it first must be defined or framed.

Conversation in this project formed a counterpoint to the visual descriptions of *tightness*. It was via informal conversation that this book was conceived, developed and finally published. Talking amongst friends and colleagues, loose and informal seems antithetical to landing definitions and precision. Yet as we have seen in the case studies, living in close proximity also requires a *loose* or open ended attitude to dialogue, as it incrementally adjusts. These texts are in part a record of conversations held during an exhibition event. Preserving the ideas contained in them as they double back, circle and construct tangents, is like a description of the *tight* city as it leaves something undone and holds onto its fragmentary qualities.

A *tight* city is one that has reconciled itself with its density – it has learned to use the space it has intelligently. Density alone does not constitute *tightness*, nor does smallness by itself. These are good starting points – not to be avoided, but *tightness* describes a set of performances rather than a physical artefact or a fixed form.

A *tight* city is one which allows for contingency and change, overlaps uses and detaches urban space from particular or prescribed functions. The physical manifestation of *tightness* are visible in concrete, everyday examples in cities. All places make these adaptations and allowances; some do so with greater intensity and with less uniformity. We have seen this with particular intensity in contemporary Asia. *Tight* form is one that has responded to physical constraint, almost to absurdity. At the same time, it embodies a kind of generosity. *Tight* form always accepts that use and occupation is possible.

Building a *tight* city is a process of constant adjustment. A *no-edit* landscape is one of constant addition and accretion. Its rules are to never delete, only to add. It relies on the undirected work of many hands, adjusting the built fabric to reconcile it with its density. It avoids the erasure of mistakes. A *supertight* city is averse to centralised planning, under singular control. It works against the concentration of capital or of space.

If *tightness* in cities has a cultural dimension, then paradoxically it requires a *looseness* of behaviour – a set of norms that will tolerate close mixing and unpredictable activity. The *loose*/*tight* binary of behaviour demands that we draw on the advantages of each; operating collectively where this is beneficial, but embracing difference to maximise our ability to adapt.

This wrests debates on urban density away from its image of conformity, control and *tight* policy, and toward the permissiveness necessary for *supertight* tactics. To live *tightly* requires a certain cultural *looseness*, and is likely essential, to *tightening* physical urban fabric.

Considerations of *tightness* also can not cease at the metropolitan limits. Understanding a *tight* city through behaviour means considering the greater hinterland that supports those behaviours and its consumption. A *tight* city does not defer or outsource to an invisible realm. Its consumption is closely coupled to the sites of production. Things made and grown for a city are *tightly* part of that city.

Supertight as a concept celebrates of the intrinsic value of living closely with others. It is an idea built into definitions of the urban, since its origin. The *tight* city has density built on desire, and there is no necessary upper limit to that desire. Even where that desire for closeness is traded against other benefits, it is weighed up on the desire to be near to, rather than to be separated from. The modern history of urban planning which sought to place limits of *tightness*, could instead see its project as facilitating the *tight*. The starting point for a discourse on the density could simply be: how much is possible, rather than how much is appropriate.

Tightness as an idea is underpinned too by a series of ethical imperatives. It is borne from asking: How much city we can really afford? In an era of environmental collapse and social isolation, both related to land consuption, the pressing answer to this question is surely less. This is not however, an argument for austerity, rather for greater variation and for saturated urban environments which are more closely concentrated together. To imagine making a *supertight* city, the starting assumption would be that people want to live close to everything and close to each other. The planning discipline's project is no longer to prevent that, but to facilitate it without limit. The new task of re-forming cities is to facilitate compression, not limit it, to find desirable ways of compressing. Most drivers for dispersing the dirty, noisy city are disappearing. Via *tightness*, density needs to be detached from its associations with scarcity, and reconnected with notions of freedom, variation and desire. Ultimately physical space is a finite resource to be distributed like any other resource. How we distribute it is crucial to the future of the earth's natural systems and to human networks. We have no desire though to resolve this discussion as closed. The *supertight* city must always, like any good conversation, to be continued.

Notes

02 Essay: Overlapping & Sharing in Tight Cities

1. refer www.photomichaelwolf.com
2. See 'Tight Density, Tight Familiarity, Overlapping City' in section 32 of this publication
3. Eric Mumford, *The CIAM Discourse on Urbanism*, 1928-1960, The MIT Press, 2000, p 85.
4. Le Corbusier & Pierre Jeanneret, 'Analysis of the fundamental elements of the "minimum house" issue', Paper presented at the *CIAM II: Die Wohnung für das Existenzminimum*, Frankfurt, 1929.
5. Nate Berg, 'William Gibson Worries Your City May Be "Cooked", www.bloomberg.com/news/articles/2012-05-08/william-gibson-worries-your-city-may-be-cooked.
6. Helier Cheung, 'Chungking Mansions: Inside Hong Kong's favourite "ghetto", https://www.bbc.com/news/world-asia-24015987.
7. The *tube house* is the common name for the very narrow tall house types in Vietnam and is a notable characteristic of the urban fabric.

07 Essay: Rasquachismo & Adjustment versus Control & Planning

1. Laura G. Gutiérrez, 'Rasquachismo', *Latina/o Studies*, edited by Deborah R. Vargas, et al., New York University Press, 2017, pp 184 -187
2. Aisha Dow, 'Motorcycles in, Cars Out', www.theage.com.au/national/victoria/motorcycles-in-cars-out-in-bold-parking-plan-for-melbournes-cbd.
3. Rasquache, www.rasquacheresidency.com/rasquachismo.
4. Yoshiharu Tsukamoto, 'Void Metabolism', *Architectural Design* September/October 2012.
5. Ibid.
6. Teiji Itoh, 'Moratorium and Invisibility', in David Stewart ed., *Arata Isozaki: Architecture 1960/1990*, exhibition catalogue of *Arata Isozaki: Architecture 1960/1990*, Tokyo, 1991, 90.

13 Essay: The Appearance of the Tight City

1. See 'Interview with New Office Works' in part 17 this publication.
2. Edward R. De Zurko, 'Alberti's Theory of Form and Function', *The Art Bulletin*, Volume 39 Issue 2, 1957, p 142.
3. From conversations with Yoshiharu Tsukamoto, 2019.
4. Ibid.

21 Essay: Situation and Desire in the Tight City

1. Feargus O'Sullivan, 'Lessons From Europe's Densest Neighborhoods', 2018, https://www.bloomberg.com/news/articles/2018-03-28/urbanist-lessons-from-the-densest-neighborhoods-across-europe.
2. Richard G. Wilkinson & Kate Pickett, 'The Spirit Level: Why More Equal Societies Almost Always Do Better', Allen Lane, 2009.
3. Andrew Stiff, 'Intimate Spaces: An Archive of Creative Observation', PhD in progress, RMIT Vietnam, 2017.
4. See 'Tight Density, Tight Familiarity, Overlapping City' in section 32 of this publication.

31 Essay: Tight & Tolerant Cultures

1. Michele Gelfand, *Rule Makers, Rule Breakers: How Tight and Loose Cultures Wire Our World*, Scribner, New York, 2018.
2. Robert Bruegmann, *Sprawl: A Compact History*, University of Chicago Press, 2008.
3. Robert Bruegmann, 'Urban Myths', 2006, https://www.theguardian.com/society/2006/jan/28/comment.
4. See Tezuka Architects, Fuji Kindergarten, Tokyo, 2007.

37 Essay: Production in Tight Cities

1. See *Hokkien Mee Diplomacy* in section 38 of this publication.
2. Marilyn A. Brown, Frank Southworth, Andrea Sarzynski, 'The Geography of Metropolitan Carbon Footprints', *Policy and Society*, Volume 27, Issue 4, 2009.
3. The concept of global ecological footprint, global hectares and all national data is sourced from the Global Footprint Network, www.footprintnetwork.org, (accessed 19 December 2020).
4. Thomas Wiedmann, Richard Wood, John Barrett, Manfred Lenzen, Richard Clay, 'The Ecological Footprint of Consumption in Victoria', 2008, library.bsl.org.au/jspui/bitstream/1/1152/1/ecological_footprint_of_Consumption_in_Victoria.pdf (accessed 20 September 2019).
5. David Moore, 'Ecological Footprint Analysis: San Francisco Oakland Freemont CA Metropolitan Statistocal Area', 2011, www.footprintnetwork.org/content/images/article_uploads/Ecological_Footprint_Analysis_San_Francisco.pdf, (accessed 19 December 2020).
6. Statistics on urban population, population density and metropolitan land area sourced from wikipedia entries for cities discussed in the essay.
7. Daisy Tam, 'Food Supply in Hong Kong', *HK Foodworks*, 19 September 2018, www.hkfoodworks.com/research/food-supply, (accessed 19 December 2020).
8. Michele J. Gelfand, *Rule Makers, Rule Breakers: How Tight and Loose Cultures Wire Our World*, Scribner, 2018
9. Nina Rappaport, 'Factory Architecture in the Age of Industry 4.0', April 19, 2017, www.metropolismag.com, (accessed 19 December 2020).
10. Nina Rappaport, *Vertical Urban Factory*, New York, Actar, 2015.
11. Graham Crist, Gretchen Wilkins, Ton Vu, *Making Vietnam*, RMIT University research report, 2015.
12. John Doyle, Graham Crist, *Farm HD*, Symposium & paper presented CUHK, 2017.
13. Hong Kong Transport Department, www.td.gov.hk/en/transport_in_hong_kong/parking/carparks, (accessed 19 December 2020).
14. See www.aerofarms.com as an example of modular growing platforms.

Image Credits

pp 4-5	Graham Crist, District 7 (2018), Digital Photograph
pp 8-9	Tobias Titz, Supertight Exhibition (2019), Digital photograph
p 15	Graham Crist, District 3 stair (2018), Digital Photograph
16-17	Vicky Jones, Supertight Exhibition (2019), Digital photograph
25	Annika Lammers, Super Tight Converstion (2019), Digital Photograph
26-27	Shiozaki Lab, Tight Density, Tight Familiarity, Overlapping City (2019), Digital Photograph
32	(Top to bottom) Ian Lambot, City of Darkness (1993) (Licensed under https://creative commons.org/licenses/by/4.0/deed.en), Digital Photograph; Matthäus Wander, hops on ground floor of w:Chungking Mansions (2013), Digital Photograph (Licensed under https://creativecommons.org/licenses/by-sa/3.0/deed.en)
33	Typical LDK Apartment plan, Ben Ellis (2021), Digital Drawing
36	(top to bottom) Graham Crist, 2J House (1993), Photograph; Baracco & Wright / Rory Gardiner, Garden House (2014), Digital Photograph; ODDO Architects, CH House (2019), Digital Photograph
39	(top to bottom) Atelier Bow Wow, House & Atelier, Tokyo (2005), Digital Photograph; Atelierco / Junpei Suzuki, Pit House in Kikuna (2021), Digital Photograph; Atelierco / Junpei Suzuki, Pit House in Kikuna (2021), Digital Photograph
41	(3 Images) WOHA, Kampung Admiralty Singapore (2017), Digital Photograph
42-43	Tohru Horiguchi, Bingo House (2021), Digital Photograph
49	Tohru Horiguchi, Bingo House (2019), Video Still Detail
50-51	Tohru Horiguchi, Bingo House (2021), Digital Photograph
53-57	(11 Images) Tohru Horiguchi, Bingo House (2019), Video Still
58-59	Minsuk Cho (Mass Studies) & Kyunsub Shin photographer, Mass Studies Office Seoul (2019), Digital Photograph
68-69	Minsuk Cho (Mass Studies), Freeze! (2019), Video Still
71 -75	(10 Images) Minsuk Cho (Mass Studies), Freeze! (2019), Video Stills
76-77	Archie Pizzini, Rasquachismo Series (2018), Digital Photograph
80	(2 Images) Archie Pizzini, Rasquachismo Series (2018), Digital Photographs
82	(Top to bottom) Archie Pizzini, Rasquachismo Series (2018), Digital Photograph; Sue Hajdu, Urban Documentation Vietnam Series (2009-2019), Digital Photograph
86-87	Sue Hajdu, Urban Documentation Vietnam Series (2009-2019), Digital Photograph
94-95	Sue Hajdu, Urban Documentation Vietnam Series (2009-2019), Digital Photograph
97 -105	(20 images) Sue Hajdu, Urban Documentation Vietnam Series (2009-2019), Digital Photographs
106-107	Archie Pizzini, Rasquachismo Series, Vietnam (2018), Digital Photograph
114-115	Archie Pizzini, Rasquachismo Series, Vietnam (2018), Digital Photograph
117-135	(22 images) Archie Pizzini, Rasquachismo Series, Vietnam (2018), Digital Photographs
134-135	RMIT Design Hub Curatorial Office, Supertight Exhibition (2019), Digital Photograph
144-145	Paul Tse & Evelyn Ting, (New Office Works), Middleman, Video Still
148	(Top to bottom) Vicky Jones, Supertight Exhibition (2019), Digital Photograph Tobias Titz, Supertight Exhibition (2019), Digital Photograph

150	(Top to bottom) Atelier Bow Wow, House Tower Tokyo (2006), Digital Photograph; Sanuki Daisuke / Hiroyuki Oki, Hem House Ho Chi Minh City (2015), Digital Photograph
152	(Top to bottom) Paul Tse & Evelyn Ting (New Office Works), Middleman (2017),Video Still; Paul Tse & Evelyn Ting (New Office Works), Shortcuts (2017), Video Still.
155	Sanuki Daisuke, Nga House (2017) Line Drawing
156-157	Tobias Titz, Supertight Exhibition (2019), Digital Photograph
159	(2 Images) Tobias Titz, Supertight Exhibition (2019), Digital Photograph
160-161	John Doyle, Supertight, Design Hub Gallery (2019) Line Drawing
162	(3 images) Doyle & Crist/RMIT Architecture, The Tight Bar (2019), Digital Drawings
164	(4 Images) Doyle & Crist/RMIT Architecture, The Tight Hem (2019), Digital Drawings
166	(4 Images) Graham Crist, Pasteur St Saigon (2018), Digital Photographs
167	(2 Images) Doyle & Crist/RMIT Architecture, The Tight Hem (2019), Digital Drawings
168	(3 Images) Graham Crist, Supertight construction, (2019), Digital Photographs
169	(2 Images) Graham Crist, Supertight events, (2019), Digital Photographs
170-171	Rafael A. Balboa (STUDIO WASABI ARCHITECTURE) with Yasemin Sahiner, Ginza, Shibuya, Shinjuku Series, Digital Image.
178-179	Rafael A. Balboa (STUDIO WASABI ARCHITECTURE) with Yasemin Sahiner, Ginza, Shibuya, Shinjuku Series, Digital Image (detail).
180-185	(4 images)Rafael A. Balboa (STUDIO WASABI ARCHITECTURE) with Yasemin Sahiner, Ginza, Shibuya, Shinjuku Series, Digital Images.
186-187	Paul Tse & Evelyn Ting (New Office Works), Growing Up Pavilion Hong Kong (2017), Digital Photograph
192-193	Paul Tse & Evelyn Ting (New Office Works) Middleman (2017),Video Still
195-203	(23 Images) Paul Tse & Evelyn Ting (New Office Works),Middleman, Short Cuts, Palm Trees (2017), Video Stills
204-205	Sanuki Daisuke/ Hiroyuki Oki, Ho Chi Minh City, Vietnam, Hem House Series (2015), Digital Photograph
209	Sanuki Daisuke / Hiroyuki Oki, Binh Thanh Houses, (2017), Digital Photograph
210-211	Sanuki Daisuke / Hiroyuki Oki, Hem House (2015), Digital Photograph
213-215	(6 Images) Sanuki Daisuke / Hiroyuki Oki, Binh Thanh Houses, (2017), Digital Photographs
216-219	(7 Images) Sanuki Daisuke / Hiroyuki Oki, Hem House (2015), Digital Photographs
220-221	(5 Images) Sanuki Daisuke / Hiroyuki Oki, Nga House (2017), Digital Photograph
222-223	Vicky Jones, Supertight Exhibition (2019), Digital Photograph
228	(Top to bottom) Walter Mittelholzer (1894-1937), Barcelona (1930), https://commons.wikimedia.org/wiki/File:ETH-BIB-Barcelona_aus _100_m_H%C3%B6he-Tschadseeflug_1930-31-LBS_MH02-08-0442.tif; Midtown manhattan Rob Snell, 2008, https://commons.wikimedia.org/wiki/ File:Midtown,_Central_Park_and_Upper_Manhattan.jpg; Mumbai 2010, MM Switzerland, https://commons.wikimedia.org/wiki/File:Mumbai_ (5356346073).jpg; Archie Pizzini, Rasquachismo Series, Vietnam (2018), Digital Photograph

230 (Top to bottom) Sue Hajdu, Urban Documentation Vietnam Series (2009-2019), Digital Photographs; Desiree Grunewald, Habitats Series (2017-2019), Digital collage; Andrew Stiff, Hem Series (2018), Video Still
232 (Top to bottom) Tohru Horiguchi, Bingo House (2019), Video Still; Shiozaki Lab, Hanami (Detail) (2019), Digital Drawing; Drawing Architecture Studio, Diamond Village (Detail) (2019), Digital Drawing
234-235 RMIT Design Hub Curatorial Office, Supertight Exhibition (2019), Digital Photograph
243 Graham Crist, Supertight Event (2019), Digital Photgraph
244-245 Superimpose, Spacious Tightness (2019), Video Still
251 Superimpose, Spacious Tightness (2019), Video Still
252-253 Superimpose, Spacious Tightness (2019), Video Still
255-261 (14 Images) Superimpose, Spacious Tightness (2019), Video Stills.
262-263 WOHA / K.Kopter, videos - Xtreme Media,Skyshot, Oasia Hotel Singapore (2016), Video Still.
265 (2 Images) WOHA / K.Kopter, videos - Xtreme Media,Skyshot, Oasia Hotel Singapore (2016), Video Still.
266-267 (4 Images) WOHA / K.Kopter, videos - Xtreme Media,Skyshot, Park Royal Hotel Pickering Singapore (2013), Video Stills.
268-269 (4 Images) WOHA / K.Kopter, videos - Xtreme Media,Skyshot, Kampung Admiralty Singapore (2017), Video Stills.
270-271 RMIT Design Hub Curatorial Office, Supertight Exhibition (2019), Digital Photograph
277 Drawing Architecture Studio, Diamond Village (2019), Digital Drawing (Detail)
278-279 Drawing Architecture Studio, Diamond Village (2019), Digital Drawing (Detail)
281 (3 Images) Drawing Architecture Studio, Diamond Village (2019), Digital Drawings (Details)
282-287 (3 images) Drawing Architecture Studio, Diamond Village (2019), Digital Drawings
288-289 Graham Crist, Tokyo Street (2018), Digital Photograph
293 Graham Crist, Gakugei-daigaku station, Tokyo (2018), Digital Photograph
294-295 RMIT Design Hub Curatorial Office, Supertight Exhibition (2019)
301 Sailko, Dharavi, (2019), https://commons.wikimedia.org/wiki/File:Dharavi,_murales_e_graffiti_02.jpg
302-303 Miho TOMINAGA (Tomito architecture) Takahito ITO (AMP/PAM), Casaco Project Series (2019), Video Still
305 (8 Images) Miho TOMINAGA (Tomito architecture) Takahito ITO (AMP/PAM), Casaco Project Series (2019), Video Stills
306-307 Miho TOMINAGA (Tomito architecture) Takahito ITO (AMP/PAM), Ecology of Casaco Project (2019), Hand Drawing
308-309 Archie Pizzini, Rasquachismo Series (2018), Digital Photograph
314 (3 Images) Archie Pizzini, Rasquachismo Series (2018), Digital Photograph
316 (3 Images) Beka & Lemoine, Moriyama San (2017), Video Stills
318-319 Vicky Jones, Supertight Exhibition (2019), Digital Photograph
325 Annika Lammers, Super Tight Converstion (2019), Digital Photograph
326-327 Shiozaki Lab, Overlapping City Installation (2019), Digital Photograph
331 (2 images) Shiozaki Lab, Capsule Hotel Series (2019), Video Stills
330-331 Shiozaki Lab, Capsule Hotel (2019), Digital Drawing
332-333 (4 images) Shiozaki Lab, Rush Hour Train Series (2019), Video Stills
334-335 Shiozaki Lab, Rush Hour Train (2019), Digital Drawing

336-337	Shiozaki Lab, Pubs Area Yokocho (2019), Digital Drawing
338	(2 images) Shiozaki Lab, Pubs Area Yokocho Series (2019), Video Stills
339	(2 images) Shiozaki Lab, Sento Series (2019), Video Stills
340-341	Shiozaki Lab, Sento (2019), Digital Drawing
342-343	(10 Images) Shiozaki Lab, Cherry-Blossom Series (2019), Video Stills
344-345	Shiozaki Lab, Cherry-Blossom Viewing (2019), Digital Drawing
346-347	(4 Images) Shiozaki Lab, Location-Based Game Series (2019), Video Stills
348-349	Shiozaki Lab, Location-Based Game (2019), Digital Drawing
350-351	Desirée Grunewald, Mapas & Habitats Series (2017-2019), Digital Photo Collage
353-369	(20 images) Desirée Grunewald, Mapas & Habitats Series (2017-2019), Digital Collage
370-371	Andrew Stiff, Zoom Series (2018), Video Still
379	Andrew Stiff, Hem Series (2018), Video Still (Detail)
380-381	Andrew Stiff, Hem Series (2018), Video Still
383-385	(5 Images) Andrew Stiff, Doan Van Do Series (2019), Video Stills
386-387	(4 Images) Andrew Stiff, Hem 42 Series (2019), Video Stills
388-389	Andrew Stiff, Hem Series (2018), Video Still
390-391	(2 Images) Andrew Stiff, Hem 84 Series (2019), Video Stills
392-399	(19 images) Andrew Stiff, HEM 243 Series (2019), Video Stills
400-401	Graham Crist, Bellarine Greenhouses (2021), Digital Photograph
406	(Top to bottom) John Doyle, Urban Footprints (2020), Digital Drawing; Charles Anderson, Alban Mannisi & Yazid bin Ninsalam, Hokkien Mee Diplomacy (2019), Video Still; Graham Crist, Saigon 2018, Digital Photograph
408	(Top to Bottom) Graham Crist, Gretchen Wilkins, Ton Vu, Making Vietnam (2016), Digital Render; John Doyle, Graham Crist, Ronald Lau & RMIT Architecture, FarmHD (2017), Digital drawing; John Doyle, Graham Crist, Ronald Lau & RMIT Architecture, FarmHD (2017), Digital Drawing
412-413	Charles Anderson, Alban Mannisi & Yazid bin Ninsalam, Hokkien Mee Diplomacy (2019), Video Still
415-417	(13 Images) Charles Anderson, Alban Mannisi & Yazid bin Ninsalam, Hokkien Mee Diplomacy (2019), Video Stills
418-419	Charles Anderson, Alban Mannisi & Yazid bin Ninsalam, Hokkien Mee Diplomacy (2019), Video Still
420-421	Vicky Jones, Supertight Exhibition (2019), Digital Photograph
425	Andrew Stiff, Hem Series detail (2018), Video Still
426-427	Vicky Jones, Supertight Exhibition (2019), Digital Photograph
428-429	RMIT Design Hub Curatorial Office, Supertight Exhibition (2019), Digital Photograph
432-433	Graham Crist, Hanoi Tight (2017), Digital Photograph
439	Andrew Stiff, HEM City Series (2017), Video Still

Note: Every effort has been made to find and seek approval from copyright holders of the images and illustrations used in this publication. In some cases creative commons licenses have be used with the specific attribution and license information contained above. Interested parties are requested to contact RMIT University School of Architecture and Urban Design.

Acknowledgments

Thanks to the many contributors to the Supertight project through its exhibition and publication.

Professor Yoshiharu Tsukamoto, who was a co-curator of the 2019 Supertight Exhibition, and whose dialogue with the project in its development was essential to its being.

Tom Muratore edited the text.

Contributors of Works:
Yoshiharu Tsukamoto / Atelier Bow-wow, Rafael A Balboa, Yasemin Sahiner, Sanuki Daisuke, Drawing Architecture Studio, Desirée Grunewald, Sue Hajdu, Professor Tohru Horiguchi, Alban Mannisi, Yazid Ninsalam, Charles Anderson, Minsuk Cho/Mass Studies, Korea, New Office Works, Archie Pizzini, Andrew Stiff, Superimpose, tomito architecture, Taishin Shiozaki, Chika Kato, Tatsuya Ide, Hyuga Obana, Li Qiaozhi, Yu Ziliang with cooperation from Taiki Hayata, Sho Tanaka, Kano Maeda, Asuka Sakurai. (Tokyo Institute of Technology/ Shiozaki Lab), Richard Hassell/WOHA, Thierry Bernard (RMIT University Vietnam),.

Exhibition Team at RMIT University Design HUB Gallery:
Kate Rhodes, Nella Themelios, Michaela Bear, Ari Sharp, Erik North, Timothy Macleod,

Funding for the project is from:
RMIT School of Architecture and Urban Design + RMIT Design Hub Gallery

Guests Conversations at the Bar Talk:
Anna Jankovic, Helen Duong, Ian Nazareth, professor Mark Jacques (Openwork, RMIT Architecture + Urban Design, Professor Nigel Bertram, Marika Neustupny (NMBW Architects, Melbourne), Aaron Roberts, Maria Luisa Nardella (City of Moreland), Ed Service (formerly City of Moreland), Luke Thornton (Beulah), Emma Jackson, Ann Lau (Director Hayball Architects), David Ma, Aleesha Callaghan & Jana Perkovic (Assemble Papers) Andy Fergus (City of Melbourne Urban Design), Katherine Sundermann (MGS architects), Alexis Kalagas, (Urban Strategist from the Urban Think Tank), Ihnji Jon (Connected Cities Mab at Melbourne University), Ishita Chatterjee (Informal Research Hub at Melbourne University), Piers Morgan (Fieldwork)

Pandarosa (exhibition graphic design); Ziga Testen (book graphic concept).

Production Assistants:
George Mollet, Amy Trethuen, Darren Soh, Megan Voo, Jin Hyung Moon, Sophie (Bao) Nguyen, Meng Xianyi, Xuanyun (Michael) Song, Annika Lammers, Bridget Foley, Hepeng Miao, Ben Ellis.

Contributors Bios

Dr. John Doyle is an architect and a partner at architecture and urban design practice Common. He is head of the Master of Architecture program at RMIT University .

Associate professor Graham Crist is an architect, director of Antarctica Architects and head of the Master of Urban Design program at RMIT University.

Tom Muratore is an architect, editor and educator based in Naarm/Melbourne.

Professor Yosiharu Tsukamoto is an architect and co-founder of Tokyo based practice Atelier Bow Wow. He is a Professor at Tokyo Institute of Technology

Taishin Shiozaki is a director of Tokyo based architecture practice Atelierco and Associate Professor at Tokyo Institute of Technology. Shiozaki Laboratory is an architecture research laboratory at Tokyo Institute of Technology founded and led by Taishin Shiozaki.

Dr. Desirée Grunewald is an illustrator and graphic artist living in Spain.

Archie Pizzini is a photographer and architect based in Vietnam, and co-founder & principal of HTA Pizzini Architects.

Rafael Balboa is an architect, founder of Studio Wasabi Tokyo and researcher at Keio University.
Yasemin Sahiner is an architect & project manager at Kengo Kuma & Associates Tokyo & Paris

New Office Works is a Hong Kong based architecture practice led by Paul Tse & Evelyn Ting
Tobias Titz is a Melbourne based photographer.

Sanuki Daisuke is an architect and founder of Sanuki Daisuke Architects in Ho Chi Minh City.
Superimpose is a Beijing based architecture practice led by Ruben Bergambagt, Carolyn Leung and Ben de Lange

WOHA is a Singapore based architecture practice founded by Wong Mun Summ & Richard Hassell.

Drawing Architecture Studio is a Beijing based practice led by Li Han & Hu Yan.The practice specialises in architecural drawing, architecural design and urban studies.

Sue Hajdu is a photographer based in Saigon, Vietnam
Andrew Stiff is a video artist, fimmaker and lecturer at RMIT University Vietnam

tomito architecture is a Tokyo based architecture practice founded by Takahito Ito & Miho Tominaga. The creators of work exhibited in this are Miho Tominaga (tomito architecture) and Takahito Ito (AMP/PAM)

Tohru Horiguchi is a scholar at Kasai University in Osaka. He is a curator of international design workshops, film screenings, lectures and events related to architecture and film.

Charles Anderson is a landscape architect and an associate professor at RMIT University.
Yazid bin Ninsalam is a landscape architect and lecturer at RMIT University.
Alban Mannisi is a landscape architect and a director at Scapethical.

Supertight:
Models for Living and Making Culture in Dense Urban Environments

Published by:
Actar Publishers, New York, Barcelona
www.actar.com

Authors: Graham Crist and John Doyle

Editing: Tom Muratore

Graphic Design: Actar with Graham Crist and John Doyle

With contributions by:
Yoshiharu Tsukamoto, Rafael A Balboa, Yasemin Sahiner, Sanuki Daisuke, Li Han, Hu Yan, Desirée Grunewald, Sue Hajdu, Tohru Horiguchi, Alban Mannisi, Yazid Ninsalam, Charles Anderson, Minsuk Cho, New Office Works, Archie Pizzini, Andrew Stiff, Superimpose, Taishin Shiozaki, WOHA

Printing and binding:Arlequin & Pierrot, Barcelona

Distribution
Actar D, Inc. New York, Barcelona.

New York
440 Park Avenue South, 17th Floor
New York, NY 10016, USA
T +1 2129662207
salesnewyork@actar-d.com

Barcelona
Roca i Batlle 2
08023 Barcelona, Spain
T +34 933 282 183
eurosales@actar-d.com

Indexing
English ISBN: 978-1-63840-006-6
Library of Congress Control Number: 2021948284

Printed in Europe
Publication date: June 2022